Mastering Python

*Advanced Programming
Techniques for Developers
Write efficient, scalable, and
modern Python applications*

THOMPSON CARTER

All rights reserved

Table of Content

TABLE OF CONTENTS

Introduction

Python is often regarded as one of the most versatile and powerful programming languages in the world. Known for its simplicity, readability, and broad range of applications, Python has become the language of choice for developers in nearly every field, from web development to data science, artificial intelligence (AI), machine learning (ML), and beyond. Over the years, Python has garnered a reputation for being easy to learn, yet powerful enough to handle the most complex and cutting-edge technologies. In this book, **Mastering Python: Advanced Programming Techniques for Developers**, we explore Python at its highest level, focusing on advanced techniques, best practices, and real-world applications across various domains.

Whether you're a seasoned developer looking to level up your skills or a beginner wanting to understand the depth and breadth of Python's capabilities, this book offers something for everyone. By delving into advanced Python topics, we aim to equip you with the knowledge and tools you need to tackle complex problems, develop sophisticated applications, and excel in the ever-evolving world of Python programming.

The Power of Python

Python's rise to prominence can be attributed to several factors: its clean syntax, extensive libraries, and the thriving community that continually contributes to its growth. From small scripts to large-scale enterprise applications, Python's ecosystem provides an extensive range of tools that make development faster, more efficient, and highly productive. Its adaptability makes it suitable for numerous domains, including web development, data analysis, automation, scientific computing, and even emerging fields like quantum computing.

This book is designed to provide an in-depth understanding of Python, its advanced concepts, and real-world applications. Each chapter tackles a significant area of Python development, offering detailed explanations, practical examples, and case studies. We cover core Python concepts, explore cutting-edge technologies, and provide solutions to challenges faced by developers today.

What You Will Learn

In this book, we begin with a deep dive into Python's core principles, helping you master the language's syntax and structure. From there, we transition to more advanced techniques like performance optimization, concurrency, and parallelism. We will explore various Python frameworks like **Django, Flask, FastAPI**, and **Pydantic**, as well as best practices for writing maintainable and scalable code. We'll discuss containerization using **Docker** and **Kubernetes**, delve into managing dependencies with **pipenv** and **virtualenv**, and explore key areas of growth like **Artificial Intelligence (AI), IoT**, and **Quantum Computing**.

Key Topics Covered:

1. **Advanced Python Programming Techniques**: We start by understanding the advanced features of Python, such as decorators, context managers, and metaclasses, and how to use them effectively in production environments.

2. **Mastering Python Libraries and Frameworks**: Learn about the most popular and powerful Python libraries and frameworks like **Django, Flask, FastAPI**, and **Pydantic**. Discover the strengths of each and how to choose the best one for your specific project.

3. **Cloud Development and Deployment**: Learn how to develop cloud-native applications using Python,

deploying them to platforms like **AWS**, **Azure**, and **Google Cloud**. We'll cover key tools like **Docker** and **Kubernetes** for deploying and scaling applications.

4. **Machine Learning and Data Science**: Python is the leading language for **machine learning** and **data science**, and we explore how to use libraries like **TensorFlow**, **scikit-learn**, and **PyTorch** for building intelligent applications. We'll discuss the fundamentals of AI and provide practical examples of using Python in real-world machine learning scenarios.

5. **Security Best Practices**: In the modern world of rapidly evolving threats, security is a key concern for developers. We'll cover common security vulnerabilities, best practices for writing secure Python code, and techniques for protecting sensitive data.

6. **The Future of Python**: With Python's role expanding into fields like AI, IoT, and quantum computing, we look at the emerging trends and technologies shaping the future of the language. We explore Python's place in these groundbreaking

areas and how you can stay ahead of the curve by embracing these technologies.

Real-World Applications

Throughout the book, we use practical, real-world examples to illustrate the techniques and concepts discussed. Whether you are building a simple web application, a complex AI model, or a cutting-edge IoT system, we provide hands-on solutions to ensure you can implement Python effectively in various use cases. We focus not only on code but also on how to build scalable, maintainable systems that can grow with your business or project needs.

In addition, we emphasize the importance of code quality, readability, and maintainability. In real-world development, writing code that is not only functional but also clean and easy to understand is essential for long-term success. By following best practices and learning from industry experts, you'll be prepared to tackle any challenge Python development throws at you.

Why This Book Is Different

Unlike other Python books that might focus on specific areas or beginner-level topics, **Mastering Python: Advanced**

Programming Techniques for Developers provides a comprehensive guide to Python's advanced features, cutting-edge frameworks, and emerging technologies. With a balanced approach that covers both theory and practical applications, this book prepares you to take your Python skills to the next level, whether you're developing high-performance systems, building AI-driven applications, or deploying cloud-based services.

In addition, the book is filled with real-world case studies, industry insights, and expert advice, making it an invaluable resource for developers looking to make an impact in modern software development.

Who Should Read This Book?

This book is aimed at developers who already have a basic understanding of Python and want to advance their skills. Whether you're working in web development, data science, machine learning, cloud computing, or systems programming, you'll find the content of this book relevant and beneficial. If you're looking to expand your expertise, tackle complex Python projects, or learn about the latest trends in Python development, this book is for you.

Conclusion

Python's ability to adapt to new challenges and technologies makes it one of the most exciting programming languages of the modern era. As a Python developer, mastering advanced techniques, frameworks, and libraries will not only make you more efficient but will also position you at the forefront of emerging fields like artificial intelligence, IoT, and quantum computing.

This book is your guide to mastering Python and becoming a more skilled and versatile developer. With comprehensive explanations, practical examples, and a focus on real-world applications, you'll be well-equipped to tackle the most advanced and exciting projects Python has to offer.

Let's dive in and begin mastering Python for the future.

CHAPTER 1

INTRODUCTION TO ADVANCED PYTHON PROGRAMMING

In this chapter, we'll lay the foundation for mastering Python at an advanced level. Whether you're a beginner transitioning into more complex concepts or an experienced developer looking to refine your skills, this chapter will guide you through the essential principles and practices that set advanced Python programming apart from beginner-level coding.

Overview of Python's Core Principles and Advanced Concepts

Python is an elegant and powerful language known for its simplicity and readability, making it an excellent choice for both beginners and advanced developers. At the core of Python lies its design philosophy—emphasizing simplicity, readability, and flexibility. However, as you progress from beginner to advanced Python development, the language's capabilities expand, allowing for more efficient and scalable software solutions.

Some of the advanced concepts you'll encounter in Python include:

- **Decorators:** Functions that modify the behavior of other functions.
- **Metaclasses:** Classes of classes that define the behavior of class creation.
- **Generators and Iterators:** Memory-efficient ways to handle large data sets.
- **Context Managers:** Techniques to manage resources like files or database connections efficiently.

Each of these concepts allows for greater flexibility and more sophisticated control over how your Python code behaves and performs.

Key Differences Between Beginner and Advanced Programming Practices

While Python's syntax is simple, mastering its deeper features requires a shift in mindset and a focus on efficiency and scalability. Here are the key differences between beginner and advanced programming practices:

- **Efficiency**: Beginners may prioritize writing code that works, but advanced developers focus on making that code run efficiently. This involves understanding time and space complexity, optimizing algorithms, and using Python's built-in libraries and tools to avoid unnecessary computation or memory usage.

- **Readability and Maintainability**: While beginners may not pay as much attention to code organization, an advanced Python developer understands the importance of writing clean, maintainable code. This includes following the Python Enhancement Proposals (PEPs), particularly PEP 8, which ensures your code is readable and consistent. Advanced developers also make use of comments, docstrings, and meaningful variable names.

- **Scalability**: As your applications grow, the ability to design scalable systems becomes essential. Beginners might create simple scripts that work for small inputs, but advanced programmers think about how their code can handle large datasets, many users, and long-running processes.

- **Design Patterns**: Beginners often rely on "trial and error," but experienced developers use established design patterns, such as the Singleton or Factory pattern, to solve recurring problems in a structured way.

The Importance of Writing Efficient, Scalable, and Maintainable Code

As you transition to advanced Python programming, the focus shifts from simply getting the code to work to ensuring that it works well under various conditions, scales to handle growing requirements, and is maintainable over time.

- **Efficiency** is crucial, especially when working with large data or building performance-critical applications. An inefficient algorithm can dramatically slow down an application or even cause it to fail under heavy load. Python provides several built-in modules, such as `timeit` and `cProfile`, that help you optimize your code for better performance.

- **Scalability** ensures that your applications can handle growth. For instance, a small web service that works perfectly with a handful of users can quickly fall apart as traffic increases. Writing scalable code often involves thinking ahead, using tools like asynchronous programming, multi-threading, and multiprocessing to avoid blocking operations and ensure smooth performance.

- **Maintainability** is key in any software project. You will often be working on large teams or revisiting projects long after the original development is complete. Writing maintainable code means adhering to coding standards, making use of version control, modularizing your code into reusable components, and using comprehensive testing to avoid bugs in the long run.

In the chapters to come, we'll dive deeper into each of these principles, breaking down Python's advanced features and providing practical examples that you can incorporate into your own work. By the end of this book, you'll be equipped with the skills to write Python code that's not only functional but also efficient, scalable, and maintainable, setting you up for success in real-world development projects.

CHAPTER 2

OPTIMIZING CODE FOR PERFORMANCE

In this chapter, we'll dive into the crucial topic of performance optimization in Python. As you advance in your Python programming journey, you'll realize that efficient code is not just about making things work—it's about making them run faster and more effectively. We will explore how to analyze and optimize the performance of your Python code and provide you with practical examples of performance bottlenecks and their solutions.

How to Analyze and Optimize the Performance of Your Python Code

Before optimizing your code, it's essential to first understand where the performance bottlenecks are. Optimization is a strategic effort, not a shot in the dark. Here's how you can analyze and improve the performance of your code:

1. **Identify Hot Spots**:

o **Profiling** is a technique that helps you identify the sections of your code that consume the most time. By profiling your code, you can focus your optimization efforts where they matter most.

2. **Optimize Algorithms**:

   o Efficiency starts with the right algorithm. Sometimes, optimizing performance is as simple as choosing a better algorithm. For example, using a sorting algorithm with a better time complexity can drastically reduce the execution time for large datasets.

3. **Memory Management**:

   o Efficient memory usage is another crucial aspect of performance. By understanding how Python manages memory (like through reference counting and garbage collection), you can write code that uses memory more effectively.

4. **Leverage Built-in Python Libraries**:

   o Python's standard library includes many optimized modules, such as `itertools` for handling iteration and `collections` for specialized data structures. Using these libraries instead of writing custom solutions can boost performance.

5. **Avoiding Common Pitfalls**:

o   Be mindful of Python's global interpreter lock (GIL), which can cause performance issues in multithreaded applications. In cases like this, using multiprocessing can be a more efficient option.

Real-World Examples of Performance Bottlenecks and Solutions

Let's look at a couple of real-world performance bottlenecks and how to solve them:

1. **Example 1: Inefficient Looping** A common performance issue in Python is the inefficient use of loops. For example, nested loops can lead to exponential time complexity, which makes your code slower as the input size increases.

   Problem:

   python

   ```python
   result = []
   for i in range(1000000):
       for j in range(1000000):
           result.append(i + j)
   ```

Solution: A better approach would be to use list comprehensions or `itertools.product` to optimize looping.

```python
import itertools
result = [sum(pair) for pair in
itertools.product(range(1000000),
repeat=2)]
```

2. **Example 2: Inefficient String Concatenation**
   Python strings are immutable, meaning each time you concatenate them, a new string object is created. In large loops, this can cause significant overhead.

   Problem:

```python
result = ""
for s in large_list_of_strings:
    result += s
```

   Solution: Instead of repeated concatenation, use a list to collect parts and then join them at the end.

```python
python
```

```
result = "".join(large_list_of_strings)
```

3. **Example 3: Excessive Memory Usage** When processing large datasets, excessive memory usage can be a problem. One example is when you're handling a large list but only need to access parts of it at a time.

Problem:

```
python


large_data = [x for x in range(1000000)]
```

Solution: Use generators to lazily load data only when needed.

```
python


large_data = (x for x in range(1000000))
```

Introduction to Profiling and Debugging Tools: cProfile and timeit

To truly optimize your Python code, you must first measure its performance. Profiling tools help you understand where your program spends the most time. Two commonly used tools in Python are `cProfile` and `timeit`.

1. **cProfile:**

   o cProfile is a built-in Python module that allows you to profile your entire program or specific functions. It shows you how much time is spent in each function, making it easy to find performance bottlenecks.

   Example:

```python
import cProfile

def slow_function():
    total = 0
    for i in range(1000000):
        total += i
    return total

cProfile.run('slow_function()')
```

   Output:

   o The output will show you the number of calls, total time, and the time spent in each function. You can use this information to identify the slowest parts of your code.

2. **timeit:**

- o timeit is useful for measuring the execution time of small code snippets. It's great for comparing the performance of different approaches to the same problem.

Example:

```python

import timeit

code1 = "sum(range(1000))"
code2 = "for i in range(1000): pass"

print(timeit.timeit(code1, number=100000))
print(timeit.timeit(code2, number=100000))
```

Output:

- o timeit will run the given code a specified number of times and return the total time taken. This allows you to compare the efficiency of different implementations.

Conclusion

Optimizing code for performance is a crucial skill for any advanced Python developer. By profiling your code, identifying bottlenecks, and making targeted improvements, you can ensure that your applications run as efficiently as possible. Real-world examples highlight how even small changes can lead to significant performance improvements. By using tools like `cProfile` and `timeit`, you can make data-driven decisions on where and how to optimize your code, ensuring it remains fast, scalable, and ready for production.

CHAPTER 3

MASTERING PYTHON DATA STRUCTURES

In this chapter, we'll explore Python's built-in data structures in detail. Python offers a rich variety of data structures that are highly efficient and flexible. Understanding when and how to use each of them is crucial for writing optimized and clean code. We'll discuss the main data structures—lists, dictionaries, sets, and tuples—and how to choose the right one for your needs. Additionally, we'll explore advanced techniques to help you make the most out of these structures in your Python programs.

Deep Dive into Python's Built-In Data Structures

Python provides four main built-in data structures: **lists**, **dictionaries**, **sets**, and **tuples**. Let's break down each of them:

1. **Lists**:
    - A list is an ordered, mutable collection of items, and it allows duplicate values.

25

- o Lists are great when you need to store ordered collections of data and need flexibility to modify them.
- o **Use cases**: Storing sequences, collections of items, or maintaining order in data.
- o **Example**:

python

```
my_list = [1, 2, 3, 4, 5]
my_list.append(6)  # Adding an item
my_list.remove(3)  # Removing an item
```

2. **Dictionaries**:

- o A dictionary is an unordered collection of key-value pairs.
- o Dictionaries are ideal when you need fast lookups based on keys and don't need the order of elements.
- o **Use cases**: Storing mappings of keys to values, such as database records or caching.
- o **Example**:

python

```
my_dict = {'name': 'Alice', 'age': 30}
```

```
my_dict['city'] = 'New York'    #
Adding a new key-value pair
del my_dict['age']  # Removing a key-
value pair
```

3. Sets:

- o A set is an unordered collection of unique elements.

- o Sets are useful when you need to store non-duplicate items and perform operations like union, intersection, and difference.

- o **Use cases**: Removing duplicates, performing mathematical set operations, or checking membership efficiently.

- o **Example**:

```python

my_set = {1, 2, 3, 4}
my_set.add(5)  # Adding an element
my_set.remove(3)    #  Removing  an
element
```

4. Tuples:

- o A tuple is an ordered, immutable collection of items. Once created, a tuple cannot be modified.

- ○ Tuples are useful when you want to ensure the immutability of your data, such as when passing data to functions or storing constant data.
- ○ **Use cases**: Storing fixed, unchanging data or creating lightweight data structures.
- ○ **Example**:

```python
python

my_tuple = (1, 2, 3)
```

Choosing the Right Data Structure for Optimal Performance

The performance of your program can often depend on the data structure you choose. Each data structure has strengths and weaknesses based on the operations you need to perform. Let's look at how to choose the right one:

1. **Lists vs Tuples**:
   - ○ **Lists** are more flexible because they allow modification (i.e., adding, removing, and changing elements).
   - ○ **Tuples**, however, are more memory-efficient because of their immutability, and their performance for certain operations (like iteration) is often faster than lists due to their fixed size.

- ○ **Best practice**: Use tuples when your data won't change, and use lists when you need to modify the collection.

2. **Dictionaries vs Lists**:
   - ○ **Dictionaries** provide faster lookups (O(1) time complexity for key access) than lists (which require O(n) time for searching through elements). If you need to access elements by a unique key, dictionaries are the go-to choice.
   - ○ **Best practice**: Use dictionaries when you need fast lookups or mapping of values, and use lists when order matters and you don't need direct key-based access.

3. **Sets vs Lists**:
   - ○ **Sets** are optimized for membership tests (O(1) time complexity), making them much faster than lists when checking for membership.
   - ○ **Best practice**: Use sets when you need to ensure uniqueness or perform set operations (union, intersection, etc.), and use lists for ordered collections where duplicates are allowed.

4. **Performance Considerations**:
   - ○ **Searching for an element**: O(n) for lists and tuples; O(1) for dictionaries and sets.
   - ○ **Insertion and deletion**: O(1) for lists (if at the end), O(n) for inserting/removing at the start or

middle; O(1) for sets and dictionaries (unless dealing with resizing).

Advanced Techniques for Using Lists, Dictionaries, Sets, and Tuples Efficiently

1. **Advanced List Techniques**:
   o **List comprehensions**: A more Pythonic and efficient way to create or filter lists.

   python

   ```
   squares = [x**2 for x in range(10)]
   ```

   o **List slicing**: Extracting portions of a list in a memory-efficient manner.

   python

   ```
   my_list = [1, 2, 3, 4, 5]
   sublist = my_list[1:4]      # Get
   elements from index 1 to 3
   ```

2. **Advanced Dictionary Techniques**:
   o **defaultdict**: A dictionary subclass that provides default values for missing keys, eliminating the need for checking key existence.

   python

30

```python
from collections import defaultdict
my_dict = defaultdict(int)
my_dict['apple'] += 1   # No need to
check if 'apple' exists
```

- o **Counter**: A specialized dictionary for counting hashable objects.

```python
from collections import Counter
word_count  =  Counter(['apple',
'banana', 'apple', 'orange'])
```

3. **Advanced Set Techniques**:
   - o **Set Comprehensions**: Create sets using comprehensions for improved readability and performance.

```python
my_set = {x**2 for x in range(10)}
```

   - o **Set Operations**: Perform efficient set operations like union, intersection, and difference.

```python
```

```
set1 = {1, 2, 3}
set2 = {3, 4, 5}
intersection = set1 & set2  # {3}
union = set1 | set2  # {1, 2, 3, 4,
5}
```

4. **Advanced Tuple Techniques**:

   o **Named Tuples**: Provide a more readable alternative to regular tuples by giving each element a name, making the code self-documenting.

   python

```
from collections import namedtuple
Point = namedtuple('Point', ['x',
'y'])
p = Point(10, 20)
print(p.x, p.y)  # Access by name
instead of index
```

Conclusion

Mastering Python's built-in data structures is essential for efficient programming. By understanding the strengths and weaknesses of lists, dictionaries, sets, and tuples, you can select the right data structure for the task at hand. In addition, leveraging advanced techniques such as list comprehensions, `defaultdict`, `Counter`, and named tuples can help you write more readable and optimized code. The key to becoming an advanced Python programmer is learning how to efficiently utilize these data structures in real-world applications, ensuring that your code remains fast, scalable, and maintainable.

CHAPTER 4

FUNCTIONAL PROGRAMMING IN PYTHON

Functional programming is a programming paradigm that treats computation as the evaluation of mathematical functions and avoids changing state and mutable data. Python supports functional programming features, allowing developers to write clean, efficient, and reusable code. In this chapter, we will dive into the key principles of functional programming and demonstrate how to apply them in Python. We will also explore higher-order functions, lambda functions, and list comprehensions, alongside real-world examples of functional programming in action.

Key Principles of Functional Programming and How to Apply Them in Python

Functional programming revolves around several core principles:

1. **First-Class Functions**:
    - o In Python, functions are first-class citizens, meaning they can be passed as arguments to other

functions, returned as values from other functions, and assigned to variables.

- o This enables more flexible and reusable code by treating functions just like other data types (e.g., integers, strings).

Example:

python

```
def add(x, y):
    return x + y

def apply_operation(func, a, b):
    return func(a, b)

result = apply_operation(add, 5, 3)    #
Result is 8
```

2. **Immutability**:

- o Functional programming emphasizes the use of immutable data. In Python, this can be achieved by using tuples, frozensets, and other immutable types.
- o Immutability ensures that data is not modified directly, making code more predictable and easier to reason about.

Example:

python

```
x = (1, 2, 3)
# x[0] = 4  # This will raise a TypeError
as tuples are immutable
```

3. **Pure Functions**:

   o A pure function is a function that always produces the same output for the same input and has no side effects (it does not alter any external state).

   o Writing pure functions helps create more predictable, testable, and debuggable code.

Example:

python

```
def square(x):
    return x * x
```

4. **Avoiding Side Effects**:

   o Functional programming aims to minimize or eliminate side effects, such as modifying global variables or altering the state of objects.

o Functions should focus on returning values based on input without changing anything outside the function.

Using Higher-Order Functions, Lambda Functions, and List Comprehensions

Now let's explore some key functional programming tools in Python: **higher-order functions**, **lambda functions**, and **list comprehensions**.

1. **Higher-Order Functions**:
   o A higher-order function is a function that either takes one or more functions as arguments or returns a function as a result.
   o Common higher-order functions in Python include `map()`, `filter()`, and `reduce()`, all of which help apply functions to iterables.

   Example: `map()`:

   o The `map()` function applies a given function to each item in an iterable (such as a list or tuple).

```python
python

def square(x):
    return x * x
```

37

```
numbers = [1, 2, 3, 4]
squares = list(map(square, numbers))  # [1,
4, 9, 16]
```

Example: `filter()`:

- o The `filter()` function filters elements from an iterable based on a condition.

```
python
```

```
def is_even(x):
    return x % 2 == 0

numbers = [1, 2, 3, 4, 5]
even_numbers     =     list(filter(is_even,
numbers))  # [2, 4]
```

Example: `reduce()`:

- o The `reduce()` function from the `functools` module applies a function cumulatively to the items of an iterable.

```
python
```

```
from functools import reduce
```

```
def multiply(x, y):
    return x * y

numbers = [1, 2, 3, 4]
product = reduce(multiply, numbers)    # 24
```

2. **Lambda Functions**:

   o   Lambda functions are small anonymous functions defined using the `lambda` keyword. They are useful when you need a simple function for a short period of time.

   o   Lambda functions can be passed as arguments to higher-order functions like `map()`, `filter()`, or `sorted()`.

Example:

```
python
```

```
# Using lambda with map
numbers = [1, 2, 3, 4]
squares = list(map(lambda x: x * x,
numbers))   # [1, 4, 9, 16]

# Using lambda with filter
even_numbers = list(filter(lambda x: x % 2
== 0, numbers))   # [2, 4]
```

Example: Sorting with lambda:

o You can also use lambda functions with the `sorted()` function to sort data based on custom criteria.

python

```
points = [(2, 3), (4, 1), (3, 5)]
sorted_points = sorted(points, key=lambda
x: x[1])   # Sort by the second value (y-
coordinate)
print(sorted_points)   # [(4, 1), (2, 3),
(3, 5)]
```

3. **List Comprehensions**:
    o List comprehensions are a concise and functional way to create lists. They allow you to transform or filter data in a readable and efficient manner.

Example:

python

```
# Creating a list of squares using list
comprehension
numbers = [1, 2, 3, 4]
squares = [x * x for x in numbers]   # [1,
4, 9, 16]
```

```
# Filtering even numbers using list
comprehension
even_numbers = [x for x in numbers if x %
2 == 0]  # [2, 4]
```

Example: Nested List Comprehensions:

o   You can also use list comprehensions in a nested
    form to handle multi-dimensional data.

python

```
matrix = [[1, 2, 3], [4, 5, 6], [7, 8, 9]]
flattened = [elem for row in matrix for
elem in row]  # [1, 2, 3, 4, 5, 6, 7, 8, 9]
```

Real-World Examples of Functional Programming in Python

1. **Functional Approach to Data Transformation**:
   Let's say you need to process a list of dictionaries
   where each dictionary contains a user's information,
   and you want to extract the user's names and ages
   and filter out any underage users.

Example:

python

```
users = [
```

41

```
    {'name': 'Alice', 'age': 30},
    {'name': 'Bob', 'age': 17},
    {'name': 'Charlie', 'age': 25}
]


# Using filter and map to extract names and
ages of users who are 18 or older
adults    =    list(map(lambda    user:
(user['name'], user['age']), filter(lambda
user: user['age'] >= 18, users)))


print(adults)        #    [('Alice',    30),
('Charlie', 25)]
```

2. **Functional Approach to String Manipulation**:
   Imagine you want to clean and format a list of email
   addresses by removing duplicates and converting
   them to lowercase.

   Example:

```python
python


emails    =        ["alice@domain.com",
"Bob@domain.com", "alice@domain.com"]


#  Removing  duplicates  using  set  and
converting to lowercase
```

```
cleaned_emails  =  list(map(lambda  email:
email.lower(), set(emails)))

print(cleaned_emails)                          #
['alice@domain.com', 'bob@domain.com']
```

Conclusion

Functional programming offers a powerful and expressive way to write clean, maintainable, and reusable code in Python. By leveraging the core principles such as first-class functions, immutability, and pure functions, along with practical tools like higher-order functions, lambda functions, and list comprehensions, you can optimize your code and solve problems more elegantly. In real-world applications, these techniques can be used to handle data transformations, process collections, and manage complex workflows in an efficient and readable manner.

CHAPTER 5

OBJECT-ORIENTED PROGRAMMING (OOP) MASTERY

Object-Oriented Programming (OOP) is a core programming paradigm in Python that allows developers to design software using objects that contain both data and methods. OOP helps in writing maintainable, reusable, and scalable code by modeling real-world entities. In this chapter, we will explore advanced OOP techniques, including inheritance, polymorphism, and composition, and examine popular design patterns in Python, such as Singleton, Factory, and Strategy patterns. We'll also look at real-world applications of OOP principles in Python projects.

Advanced OOP Techniques: Inheritance, Polymorphism, and Composition

1. **Inheritance**:

    o   Inheritance allows a class (the subclass) to inherit properties and methods from another class (the superclass). This promotes code reuse and a hierarchical class structure.

- o Inheritance can be **single** or **multiple**, but Python supports single inheritance by default and allows multiple inheritance with some precautions.

Example:

```python

class Animal:
    def speak(self):
        raise
NotImplementedError("Subclass        must
implement abstract method")

class Dog(Animal):
    def speak(self):
        return "Woof!"

class Cat(Animal):
    def speak(self):
        return "Meow!"

dog = Dog()
cat = Cat()
print(dog.speak())  # Woof!
print(cat.speak())  # Meow!
```

2. **Polymorphism**:
   - Polymorphism allows different classes to implement the same method in a way that is suited to each class. This allows for interchangeable objects, enhancing code flexibility.
   - Polymorphism in Python is often achieved through method overriding (like in the example above) or through duck typing, where the behavior of an object is determined by its methods and properties rather than its class.

Example:

python

```python
class Bird:
    def fly(self):
        return "Flying high"

class Airplane:
    def fly(self):
        return "Flying at 30,000 feet"

def let_it_fly(flyable):
    print(flyable.fly())

bird = Bird()
```

```
airplane = Airplane()
let_it_fly(bird)  # Flying high
let_it_fly(airplane)  # Flying at 30,000
feet
```

3. **Composition**:

   o Composition is a design principle where one class contains instances of other classes to build more complex functionality. It promotes code reuse by delegating tasks to other objects.

   o Composition is often favored over inheritance because it provides greater flexibility and reduces the complexity of class hierarchies.

Example:

python

```
class Engine:
    def start(self):
        return "Engine started"

class Car:
    def __init__(self, engine):
        self.engine = engine

    def drive(self):
        return f"Car is moving. {self.engine.start()}"
```

47

```
engine = Engine()
car = Car(engine)
print(car.drive())  # Car is moving. Engine
started
```

Design Patterns in Python: Singleton, Factory, and Strategy

Design patterns are reusable solutions to common problems in software design. Python, like many object-oriented languages, benefits from using design patterns to structure code in a more maintainable and extensible way.

1. **Singleton Pattern**:
   o The Singleton pattern ensures that a class has only one instance and provides a global point of access to it. This is useful when you need to manage shared resources, such as a configuration manager or a database connection.

   Example:

```python

class Singleton:
    _instance = None

    def __new__(cls):
        if cls._instance is None:
```

```
        cls._instance              =
super(Singleton, cls).__new__(cls)
        return cls._instance

instance1 = Singleton()
instance2 = Singleton()
print(instance1 is instance2)  # True, both
are the same instance
```

2. **Factory Pattern**:

  o The Factory pattern is used to create objects without specifying the exact class of the object that will be created. It provides a method for creating objects based on conditions, such as type or user input, without exposing the creation logic.

Example:

```python

class Dog:
    def speak(self):
        return "Woof!"


class Cat:
    def speak(self):
        return "Meow!"


class AnimalFactory:
```

```
@staticmethod
def create_animal(animal_type):
    if animal_type == 'dog':
        return Dog()
    elif animal_type == 'cat':
        return Cat()

animal                              =
AnimalFactory.create_animal('dog')
print(animal.speak())  # Woof!
```

3. **Strategy Pattern**:

- o The Strategy pattern allows a method to have different behaviors depending on the context, enabling the dynamic change of algorithms or behaviors without changing the client code.
- o In Python, the Strategy pattern can be implemented by passing different strategy objects to a context object, allowing behavior to change at runtime.

Example:

```
python

class Strategy:
    def execute(self):
        pass
```

```python
class AddStrategy(Strategy):
    def execute(self, a, b):
        return a + b

class SubtractStrategy(Strategy):
    def execute(self, a, b):
        return a - b

class Calculator:
    def __init__(self, strategy: Strategy):
        self.strategy = strategy

    def calculate(self, a, b):
        return self.strategy.execute(a, b)

# Using different strategies
add = AddStrategy()
subtract = SubtractStrategy()

calculator = Calculator(add)
print(calculator.calculate(5, 3))  # 8

calculator.strategy = subtract
print(calculator.calculate(5, 3))  # 2
```

Real-World Applications of OOP Principles in Python Projects

1. **Web Application Development (Django/Flask)**:

51

- o OOP principles, particularly inheritance and composition, are widely used in web frameworks like Django and Flask. Django's class-based views and model system rely heavily on inheritance to allow developers to extend existing functionality.

Example (Django Model Inheritance):

```python

from django.db import models

class Animal(models.Model):
    name                              =
models.CharField(max_length=100)

class Dog(Animal):
    breed                             =
models.CharField(max_length=100)

# Here, Dog inherits properties from
Animal, enabling code reuse
```

2. **Game Development (Pygame)**:
   - o Game development often involves complex hierarchies of objects, such as different types of characters, enemies, and obstacles. By using

inheritance, polymorphism, and composition, you can easily extend and modify game logic.

Example (Pygame Character Inheritance):

python

```
class Character:
    def __init__(self, name):
        self.name = name

    def attack(self):
        print(f"{self.name} attacks!")

class Warrior(Character):
    def attack(self):
        print(f"{self.name}    swings    a
sword!")

warrior = Warrior("Conan")
warrior.attack()   # Conan swings a sword!
```

3. **Simulation Systems**:

   o In simulation systems, objects often need to interact with each other and can be composed of smaller components. For example, in a traffic simulation, cars can be objects composed of a speedometer and a GPS system.

Example (Simulation Composition):

python

```
class GPS:
    def get_location(self):
        return "51.5074N, 0.1278W"

class Car:
    def __init__(self, gps):
        self.gps = gps

    def get_position(self):
        return self.gps.get_location()

gps = GPS()
car = Car(gps)
print(car.get_position())    #  51.5074N,
0.1278W
```

Conclusion

Mastering Object-Oriented Programming in Python is essential for building scalable, maintainable, and extensible software. Advanced OOP techniques such as inheritance, polymorphism, and composition enable you to create complex systems with clean, reusable code. Design patterns like Singleton, Factory, and Strategy help solve common problems with proven solutions. Whether you're developing web applications, games, or simulations, applying OOP principles in Python will allow you to build robust and efficient software solutions.

CHAPTER 6

ASYNCHRONOUS PROGRAMMING WITH PYTHON

Asynchronous programming allows you to write programs that can handle multiple tasks simultaneously without blocking the execution of other tasks. This is particularly useful when working with I/O-bound operations, such as web requests, file I/O, or database queries. In this chapter, we'll introduce you to the concepts of `async` and `await` for non-blocking operations, how to write asynchronous code using Python's `asyncio` library, and practical applications like web scraping and interacting with APIs.

Introduction to `async` and `await` for Non-Blocking Operations

1. **Why Asynchronous Programming?**

   o In traditional, synchronous programming, each operation is performed one after another, blocking the program until the current operation finishes. This becomes inefficient, especially when dealing with I/O-bound tasks like network requests or reading files.

- o Asynchronous programming allows your program to perform other tasks while waiting for an I/O operation to complete. This improves performance and responsiveness, especially in programs that need to handle many I/O operations concurrently.

2. **Understanding `async` and `await`:**

   - o Python introduced `async` and `await` in Python 3.5 to make it easier to write asynchronous code.
     - **`async`** is used to define a coroutine function that will be executed asynchronously.
     - **`await`** is used inside a coroutine to pause its execution until the result of an asynchronous operation is ready.
   - o These keywords allow Python to schedule and run I/O-bound tasks concurrently, making your program more efficient without the need for complex threading.

Example:

```python
import asyncio

async def say_hello():
```

```
print("Hello")
await asyncio.sleep(1)    # Simulates a
non-blocking delay
print("World")

# Run the asynchronous function
asyncio.run(say_hello())
```

In this example, `asyncio.sleep(1)` is a non-blocking operation, so while Python waits for the sleep to finish, other tasks can be executed. The program doesn't freeze during this waiting time.

How to Write Asynchronous Code Using `asyncio` and `aiohttp`

1. **Using `asyncio` for Asynchronous Programming**:

   o `asyncio` is a Python library that provides tools for writing asynchronous programs. It allows you to manage tasks concurrently and is built around coroutines, events, and the event loop.

   o **Creating Coroutines**:

      ▪ Coroutines are special functions defined using `async def`, and they can be awaited using the `await` keyword.

   Example:

```python
python

import asyncio

async def download_data(url):
    print(f"Downloading data from
{url}")
    await asyncio.sleep(2)       #
Simulate a network request
    print(f"Downloaded data from
{url}")

async def main():
    await asyncio.gather(

download_data("https://example.com/
1"),

download_data("https://example.com/
2"),

download_data("https://example.com/
3")
    )

asyncio.run(main())
```

In this example, three download tasks are executed concurrently, without blocking each other. The program waits for all tasks to complete before finishing.

2. **Using `aiohttp` for Asynchronous HTTP Requests**:

   o `aiohttp` is an asynchronous HTTP client and server for Python. It's built on top of `asyncio` and allows you to make HTTP requests asynchronously, making it perfect for tasks like web scraping or interacting with APIs.

   Example: Asynchronous Web Scraping with `aiohttp`:

   python

   ```python
   import aiohttp
   import asyncio

   async def fetch_page(url):
       async with aiohttp.ClientSession() as session:
           async with session.get(url) as response:
               page_content = await response.text()
   ```

```
        print(f"Fetched content from
{url}     (size:     {len(page_content)}
characters)")

async def main():
    urls = [
        "https://example.com/page1",
        "https://example.com/page2",
        "https://example.com/page3"
    ]
    tasks = [fetch_page(url) for url in
urls]
    await asyncio.gather(*tasks)

asyncio.run(main())
```

In this example, `aiohttp` is used to fetch multiple web pages concurrently. Each `session.get()` call is non-blocking, so the program can make multiple requests at the same time, significantly reducing the overall execution time compared to sequential requests.

Real-World Scenarios for Using Asynchronous Programming

1. **Web Scraping**:
   - o Web scraping involves fetching web pages and extracting data from them. Asynchronous

programming is ideal for web scraping because it allows you to make many HTTP requests simultaneously, drastically speeding up the scraping process. Tools like `aiohttp` and `BeautifulSoup` can be combined to scrape data efficiently.

Example (real-world scenario):

```python
import aiohttp
from bs4 import BeautifulSoup
import asyncio

async def fetch_and_parse(url):
    async with aiohttp.ClientSession() as session:
        async with session.get(url) as response:
            page_content = await response.text()
            soup = BeautifulSoup(page_content, 'html.parser')
            title = soup.find('title').get_text()
            print(f"Page Title from {url}: {title}")
```

```python
async def main():
    urls     =     ["https://example.com",
"https://example.org"]
    tasks = [fetch_and_parse(url) for url
in urls]
    await asyncio.gather(*tasks)

asyncio.run(main())
```

In this scenario, asynchronous programming is used to fetch and parse multiple web pages concurrently, making the scraping process much faster than using a synchronous approach.

2. **Interacting with APIs**:

   o Asynchronous programming is useful when interacting with APIs, especially if you need to make many requests (e.g., fetching data from multiple endpoints or handling large-scale data).

   o With `aiohttp`, you can interact with RESTful APIs or any other web services asynchronously.

Example (interacting with a public API):

```python
python

import aiohttp
import asyncio
```

```python
async def get_weather(city):
    api_url                        =
f"http://api.openweathermap.org/data/2.5/
weather?q={city}&appid=your_api_key"
    async with aiohttp.ClientSession() as
session:
        async with session.get(api_url) as
response:
            data = await response.json()
            print(f"Weather   in   {city}:
{data['weather'][0]['description']}")

async def main():
    cities  =  ["London",  "New  York",
"Tokyo"]
    tasks = [get_weather(city) for city in
cities]
    await asyncio.gather(*tasks)

asyncio.run(main())
```

In this example, the program fetches weather data for multiple cities concurrently from the OpenWeather API, making the process faster and more efficient compared to sequential requests.

3. **Background Tasks and Periodic Jobs**:

- o Asynchronous programming can be used for background tasks and periodic jobs, such as sending email notifications, processing data in batches, or regularly checking for new information in a database or file system.
- o Python's `asyncio` and `aiohttp` can be combined with tools like `APScheduler` or `Celery` to manage and schedule asynchronous tasks.

Conclusion

Asynchronous programming is a powerful tool for handling I/O-bound operations in Python. By using `async` and `await` in combination with libraries like `asyncio` and `aiohttp`, you can write highly efficient, non-blocking code that performs multiple tasks concurrently. This is especially useful in real-world applications like web scraping, API interactions, and managing background tasks. By mastering asynchronous programming, you can improve the performance of your Python applications, making them faster and more responsive, even under heavy loads.

CHAPTER 7

CONCURRENCY AND PARALLELISM

Concurrency and parallelism are essential concepts in computer science, especially in Python, where you may need to execute multiple tasks simultaneously for efficiency. While they sound similar, concurrency and parallelism have distinct meanings and use cases. In this chapter, we'll discuss the differences between concurrency and parallelism, explore how to leverage Python's threading, multiprocessing, and asyncio libraries to scale applications, and look at real-world examples of using concurrency and parallelism to improve performance.

Differences Between Concurrency and Parallelism

1. **Concurrency**:
    o Concurrency is about dealing with multiple tasks at the same time, but not necessarily executing them simultaneously. It allows a program to make progress on multiple tasks, switching between them, without having to wait for each task to finish before starting another.

- o In a **concurrent program**, the tasks may be run in a single core, with the operating system or interpreter switching between them, giving the illusion of simultaneous execution. However, only one task is executed at any given moment, just rapidly switching between them.

Example:

- o Imagine a waiter taking multiple orders in a restaurant: the waiter serves multiple tables, but only one order is being processed at a time, with the waiter switching between them.

2. **Parallelism**:
   - o Parallelism, on the other hand, refers to executing multiple tasks simultaneously, typically on multiple cores or processors. The tasks are truly running at the same time, and they are divided into smaller sub-tasks that can be executed in parallel.
   - o In a **parallel program**, tasks are split into smaller units that run simultaneously, speeding up the overall processing, especially for CPU-bound tasks.

Example:

o The parallel equivalent of the waiter would be multiple waiters serving tables at the same time, each handling a separate order.

In summary, **concurrency** involves managing multiple tasks by interleaving their execution, while **parallelism** involves executing multiple tasks simultaneously.

How to Leverage Threading, Multiprocessing, and Asyncio to Scale Applications

1. **Threading**:

   o Threading allows you to run multiple tasks concurrently within a single process. However, because of Python's Global Interpreter Lock (GIL), threading is not ideal for CPU-bound tasks, but it can be effective for I/O-bound tasks.

   o Threading is most commonly used when you need to perform many I/O-bound operations concurrently, such as network requests or file operations.

   Example (Threading):

```python
import threading
import time
```

```
def print_numbers():
    for i in range(5):
        print(i)
        time.sleep(1)

def print_letters():
    for letter in "ABCDE":
        print(letter)
        time.sleep(1)

thread1                                    =
threading.Thread(target=print_numbers)
thread2                                    =
threading.Thread(target=print_letters)

thread1.start()
thread2.start()

thread1.join()
thread2.join()
```

In this example, both functions will run concurrently, interleaving their outputs, but since Python's GIL prevents true parallel execution of CPU-bound tasks, threading is ideal for I/O-bound operations like waiting for data from a network.

2. **Multiprocessing**:

o Multiprocessing allows you to run multiple processes, each with its own Python interpreter and memory space, so it can fully utilize multiple CPU cores. Unlike threading, multiprocessing bypasses the GIL, making it an ideal solution for CPU-bound tasks.

o This approach is well-suited for tasks that involve heavy computation, such as data processing, machine learning, or simulations.

Example (Multiprocessing):

```python
python

import multiprocessing
import time

def compute_square(number):
    print(f"The square of {number} is {number**2}")
    time.sleep(1)

if __name__ == "__main__":
    processes = []
    for i in range(5):
        process = multiprocessing.Process(target=compute_square, args=(i,))
        processes.append(process)
```

```
process.start()

for process in processes:
    process.join()
```

In this example, the `compute_square` function runs in parallel across multiple processes, utilizing multiple CPU cores for faster execution of CPU-bound tasks.

3. **Asyncio**:
   - `asyncio` is a library for asynchronous programming that runs concurrently using coroutines. It's ideal for I/O-bound tasks and is especially useful for managing hundreds or thousands of tasks that involve waiting for external events, such as network requests or database queries, without blocking the program.
   - Unlike threading, `asyncio` uses an event loop to manage tasks and executes them one at a time, but it gives the illusion of concurrent execution by pausing one task when it's waiting (e.g., for I/O) and running another task in the meantime.

Example (Asyncio):

```python
python
```

71

```python
import asyncio

async def fetch_data(url):
    print(f"Fetching data from {url}")
    await asyncio.sleep(2)    # Simulate network delay
    print(f"Finished fetching data from {url}")

async def main():
    urls = ["https://example.com/1", "https://example.com/2", "https://example.com/3"]
    tasks = [fetch_data(url) for url in urls]
    await asyncio.gather(*tasks)

asyncio.run(main())
```

In this example, three network requests are handled concurrently, but the program doesn't block when waiting for data. Instead, the event loop moves on to the next task.

Real-World Examples of Using Concurrency and Parallelism to Improve Performance

1. **Web Scraping (Concurrency with Asyncio):**

o Suppose you need to scrape data from several websites concurrently. Using `asyncio` and `aiohttp` allows you to make asynchronous HTTP requests, significantly speeding up the process compared to sequential scraping.

Example:

```python
python

import aiohttp
import asyncio

async def fetch_page(url):
    async with aiohttp.ClientSession() as session:
        async with session.get(url) as response:
            return await response.text()

async def main():
    urls = ["https://example.com",
"https://example.org",
"https://example.net"]
    tasks = [fetch_page(url) for url in urls]
    html_pages = await asyncio.gather(*tasks)
    for page in html_pages:
```

73

```
    print(f"Fetched         {len(page)}
characters")
```

```
asyncio.run(main())
```

In this example, the program fetches multiple pages concurrently, cutting down the total time compared to running the requests sequentially.

2. **Image Processing (Parallelism with Multiprocessing)**:

   o If you need to apply an image filter to a large batch of images, parallelizing the image processing using `multiprocessing` can dramatically reduce the overall processing time, especially if you have multiple CPU cores available.

Example:

```python
from multiprocessing import Pool
from PIL import Image

def process_image(image_path):
    with Image.open(image_path) as img:
```

```
        img = img.convert('L')   # Convert
to grayscale

img.save(f"processed_{image_path}")

if __name__ == '__main__':
    image_paths    =    ["image1.jpg",
"image2.jpg", "image3.jpg", "image4.jpg"]
    with Pool(processes=4) as pool:
        pool.map(process_image,
image_paths)
```

In this example, the images are processed in parallel, with each image being handled by a separate process. This significantly speeds up the image processing for large datasets.

3. **Real-Time Data Processing (Threading)**:
   o If you're building a real-time data processing application, such as a chat server or a live data feed, you might want to handle incoming connections and processing concurrently. Threading can help by allowing each connection to be handled by a separate thread, enabling your application to scale without blocking other tasks.

Example:

```python
python

import threading
import time

def process_data(connection):
    print(f"Processing          connection
{connection}")
    time.sleep(2)   # Simulate processing
time
    print(f"Finished processing connection
{connection}")

connections = [1, 2, 3, 4, 5]
threads = []

for connection in connections:
    thread                          =
threading.Thread(target=process_data,
args=(connection,))
    threads.append(thread)
    thread.start()

for thread in threads:
    thread.join()
```

Here, each connection is handled in a separate thread, allowing the server to process multiple connections concurrently without waiting for each one to finish before starting another.

Conclusion

Understanding the differences between concurrency and parallelism, and knowing how to use Python's threading, multiprocessing, and asyncio libraries, is essential for writing scalable, high-performance applications. By leveraging these tools, you can handle multiple tasks concurrently or in parallel, improving the efficiency of your applications. Whether you're working with I/O-bound tasks, CPU-bound tasks, or real-time systems, using concurrency and parallelism correctly can lead to significant performance improvements.

CHAPTER 8

WORKING WITH DATABASES AND ORM

In modern software development, databases are at the heart of most applications. Whether you are building a small web app or a large-scale enterprise system, understanding how to work with relational and NoSQL databases is essential. In this chapter, we will explore how to interact with databases in Python, how to use Object-Relational Mappers (ORMs) like SQLAlchemy, and real-world examples of building scalable applications with a database backend.

Overview of Working with Relational and NoSQL Databases in Python

1. **Relational Databases (RDBMS)**:
   - o Relational databases store data in tables, which are linked by relationships. These databases use SQL (Structured Query Language) for querying and managing data. Examples of relational databases include **MySQL**, **PostgreSQL**, **SQLite**, and **SQL Server**.

- o In a relational database, data is structured in rows and columns, and tables are related to each other via primary and foreign keys.
- o Common tasks when working with relational databases in Python include creating tables, inserting records, querying data, updating data, and deleting records.

Example (SQL Query in Python using SQLite):

```python
import sqlite3

# Connect to a SQLite database (or create
it if it doesn't exist)
conn = sqlite3.connect('example.db')
cursor = conn.cursor()

# Create a table
cursor.execute('''CREATE    TABLE    IF    NOT
EXISTS users (id INTEGER PRIMARY KEY, name
TEXT, age INTEGER)''')

# Insert data
cursor.execute("INSERT  INTO  users  (name,
age) VALUES (?, ?)", ("Alice", 30))

# Query data
```

79

```
cursor.execute("SELECT * FROM users")
print(cursor.fetchall())   # Output: [(1,
'Alice', 30)]


# Commit changes and close the connection
conn.commit()
conn.close()
```

2. **NoSQL Databases**:

   o NoSQL databases are used for storing unstructured data that does not fit neatly into tables. They are more flexible and scale better horizontally than relational databases.

   o Common types of NoSQL databases include **Document Stores** (e.g., MongoDB), **Key-Value Stores** (e.g., Redis), **Column-Family Stores** (e.g., Cassandra), and **Graph Databases** (e.g., Neo4j).

   o NoSQL databases are typically used for large-scale applications, such as real-time web apps, IoT systems, and big data analytics.

   Example (Using MongoDB with Python):

```
python


from pymongo import MongoClient
```

```
# Connect to MongoDB (default is
localhost:27017)
client                              =
MongoClient('mongodb://localhost:27017/')
db = client['example_db']
collection = db['users']

# Insert data
collection.insert_one({"name":    "Alice",
"age": 30})

# Query data
user     =     collection.find_one({"name":
"Alice"})
print(user)  # Output: {'_id': ..., 'name':
'Alice', 'age': 30}
```

o **Advantages of NoSQL**:

- Flexible schema (data can be stored in various formats like JSON or BSON).
- High scalability, ideal for large applications with distributed data.
- Handles complex, hierarchical data well (e.g., social networks).

How to Use Object-Relational Mappers (ORMs) like SQLAlchemy

An Object-Relational Mapper (ORM) is a programming technique that allows you to interact with relational databases using object-oriented programming languages like Python. Instead of writing raw SQL queries, you use Python classes and objects to interact with the database. This allows for more readable, maintainable code, and helps abstract away the details of database interactions.

SQLAlchemy is the most popular ORM in Python, and it provides tools for both simple and advanced database interaction.

1. **Setting Up SQLAlchemy**:
   - o SQLAlchemy provides a high-level API to connect to the database, define tables as Python classes, and perform queries in an object-oriented way.

   Basic Setup with SQLAlchemy:

   python

```
from sqlalchemy import create_engine,
Column, Integer, String
from sqlalchemy.ext.declarative import
declarative_base
from sqlalchemy.orm import sessionmaker

# Create an engine to connect to the
database (SQLite in this case)
```

```python
engine                                    =
create_engine('sqlite:///example.db',
echo=True)

# Declare the base class
Base = declarative_base()

# Define the User class (this will map to
the 'users' table)
class User(Base):
    __tablename__ = 'users'
    id = Column(Integer, primary_key=True)
    name = Column(String)
    age = Column(Integer)

# Create the table in the database
Base.metadata.create_all(engine)

# Create a session
Session = sessionmaker(bind=engine)
session = Session()

# Insert data into the database
new_user = User(name="Alice", age=30)
session.add(new_user)
session.commit()

# Query data from the database
users = session.query(User).all()
```

```
print(users)                    #          Output:
[<User(name='Alice', age=30)>]


# Close the session
session.close()
```

2. **Using SQLAlchemy ORM Features**:
   o **CRUD Operations**:
     ▪ Create, Read, Update, and Delete operations are abstracted as methods in SQLAlchemy, making database interaction more intuitive.

Create:

```python
new_user = User(name="Bob", age=25)
session.add(new_user)
session.commit()
```

Read:

```python
users                                    =
session.query(User).filter_by(name="Alice
").all()
```

Update:

python

```
user                                    =
session.query(User).filter_by(name="Bob")
.first()
user.age = 26
session.commit()
```

Delete:

python

```
user                                    =
session.query(User).filter_by(name="Alice
").first()
session.delete(user)
session.commit()
```

3. **Relationships and Joins**:
   o   SQLAlchemy allows you to define relationships between tables, such as one-to-many or many-to-many, and automatically generates SQL joins.

Example (One-to-Many Relationship):

python

```python
from sqlalchemy import ForeignKey
from sqlalchemy.orm import relationship

class Post(Base):
    __tablename__ = 'posts'
    id = Column(Integer, primary_key=True)
    title = Column(String)
    user_id       =       Column(Integer,
ForeignKey('users.id'))


    user       =       relationship("User",
back_populates="posts")

User.posts       =       relationship("Post",
order_by=Post.id, back_populates="user")

# Create the tables
Base.metadata.create_all(engine)

# Add a user and some posts
user = User(name="Alice", age=30)
post1 = Post(title="Post 1", user=user)
post2 = Post(title="Post 2", user=user)

session.add(user)
session.commit()
```

Real-World Examples of Building Scalable Applications with a
Database Backend

1. **Building a Scalable Web Application**:
   - ○ A web application like a blog or e-commerce site can leverage SQLAlchemy to handle users, posts, and product catalogs. By using an ORM, developers can easily map entities like users and products to tables and perform CRUD operations efficiently.

   Example: Blog System:

   - ○ You can create tables for `users`, `posts`, and `comments` with relationships between them. This allows you to scale the system by adding new features, like adding a "like" system or managing a shopping cart.

2. **Building a Scalable Analytics System**:
   - ○ For an analytics platform that processes large volumes of data, SQLAlchemy can be used to interact with a relational database for structured data storage, while a NoSQL database like MongoDB could store unstructured logs.
   - ○ Python's `pandas` library could be used for handling data frames, and the ORM helps by

abstracting database interactions, making the code more maintainable and readable.

Example: Data Collection and Reporting:

o Collect data from various sensors (stored in a relational database) and process this data for reporting or visualization.

3. **Social Media Application**:
   o In a social media app, SQLAlchemy could be used to define relationships between `users`, `posts`, and `comments`. These models can be easily scaled as the application grows. Additional features, like followers, likes, and tags, can be added by expanding the database schema and leveraging the ORM to interact with the database.

Conclusion

Working with databases is a key part of modern application development. Understanding both relational and NoSQL databases, and using Object-Relational Mappers (ORMs) like SQLAlchemy, helps streamline database interactions, making it easier to scale applications. ORMs abstract away raw SQL queries, making code cleaner and more maintainable, while also offering advanced features like relationships, migrations, and transaction management. Whether you're building a small blog or a large social network, knowing how to work effectively with databases is crucial for developing robust, scalable systems.

CHAPTER 9

DESIGNING SCALABLE PYTHON APPLICATIONS

Scalability is one of the most critical factors in designing modern applications. It refers to the ability of a system to handle an increasing amount of load or expand to accommodate growth in data, traffic, or functionality without compromising performance. In this chapter, we will explore the core principles of scalable application design, strategies for managing large systems, and real-world case studies of scalable Python applications across different industries.

Principles of Scalable Application Design

When designing scalable Python applications, the goal is to ensure that the system can handle growth efficiently while maintaining optimal performance. Here are the key principles to consider:

1. **Modularity**:
   o Break down the application into smaller, independent components or services that can be

developed, tested, and scaled individually. This is commonly achieved using a **microservices architecture**, where each service is responsible for a specific piece of functionality.

o   By decoupling the application into modules, you can scale individual parts as needed without scaling the entire system.

Example:

o   In a social media application, the user authentication system, content feed generation, and notification system can all be implemented as separate services, each scaled independently.

2. **Separation of Concerns**:

o   Ensure that each component or module of your application has a well-defined responsibility and does not interfere with other parts of the system. This minimizes dependencies and ensures that changes in one module don't affect others.

o   For example, separating your business logic from the data access layer ensures that changes in how data is stored or accessed don't affect the overall application functionality.

3. **Efficient Data Management**:

o   As your application scales, the amount of data it processes and stores will grow. Efficient data management techniques, such as **caching**, **database indexing**, and **denormalization**, are essential to handle larger datasets efficiently.

o Caching frequently accessed data (e.g., user profiles, product information) using tools like **Redis** can significantly reduce database load and improve response times.

Example:

o For an e-commerce application, caching the product catalog in memory can reduce the need to query the database on every page load, speeding up the user experience.

4. **Load Balancing**:

o Distribute traffic evenly across multiple instances of your application to ensure no single server is overwhelmed. **Load balancers** can be used to route requests to different servers based on factors like server health, capacity, or geographic location.

o Horizontal scaling (adding more servers) is commonly used in scalable applications to ensure high availability and fault tolerance.

Example:

o   For a high-traffic web application, using load balancers to distribute incoming requests across multiple web servers ensures that no single server is overwhelmed, maintaining fast response times during peak hours.

5. **Asynchronous Programming**:

o   Using **asynchronous programming** techniques allows your application to perform non-blocking operations (such as I/O operations, network requests, etc.) without waiting for tasks to complete. This improves the system's responsiveness and enables it to handle many tasks concurrently.

o   Python's **asyncio** library is an excellent tool for managing asynchronous I/O-bound tasks, while **Celery** can be used for distributing background tasks.

6. **Elasticity**:

o   A scalable application should be able to scale up or down based on demand. Using cloud services like **AWS**, **Azure**, or **Google Cloud**, you can automatically scale resources based on traffic, ensuring that you only use what you need, when you need it.

o   Elasticity is important for reducing costs and improving system reliability. Auto-scaling ensures that your application doesn't experience downtime during traffic spikes and reduces overhead when traffic is low.

Example:

- o In an online media platform, you may use auto-scaling to ensure that extra compute power is provisioned during a live streaming event, and scale down when the event ends.

7. **Fault Tolerance and Redundancy**:
   - o A scalable application should be designed to be resilient, with the ability to recover from failures without affecting users. Implement redundancy and failover mechanisms to ensure high availability.
   - o Implement **database replication** and **data backups**, and design the system so that it can recover gracefully from unexpected failures.

Strategies for Managing Large Applications and Systems

Managing large-scale applications involves organizing the codebase, infrastructure, and team workflows to ensure efficiency, maintainability, and scalability. Below are several strategies to consider:

94

1. **Microservices Architecture**:
    - As applications grow, maintaining a monolithic codebase becomes cumbersome. A **microservices architecture** decomposes the system into smaller, independent services that can be developed, deployed, and scaled independently.
    - Each microservice is responsible for a specific functionality (e.g., user authentication, product catalog, payment processing). Communication between services is often achieved via lightweight protocols like **HTTP REST APIs** or **message queues** (e.g., RabbitMQ, Kafka).

    Example:

    - An e-commerce platform might have separate microservices for the cart system, user profile management, and payment processing. This allows each service to be scaled independently based on its load.

2. **Containerization**:
    - Use **Docker** to containerize applications, enabling them to run consistently across different environments. Containers make it easier to scale applications, isolate services, and deploy them in

different environments (e.g., local, staging, production).

o   Container orchestration tools like **Kubernetes** help manage containerized applications at scale by automating deployment, scaling, and operations.

Example:

o   A cloud-based application can use Kubernetes to manage containers for the front-end, back-end, and database services, ensuring that resources are efficiently allocated and scaled as needed.

3. **Event-Driven Architecture**:

o   An event-driven approach enables communication between components through asynchronous events. This is especially useful for decoupling services and scaling systems based on events.

o   **Event queues** (e.g., Kafka, AWS SQS) allow different services to react to and process events without directly communicating with each other, enabling loose coupling and better fault tolerance.

Example:

- In a social media platform, when a user posts content, an event is triggered. Different services (like notifications, content moderation, and analytics) can react to this event without direct coupling.

4. **Continuous Integration and Continuous Deployment (CI/CD):**
   - As your application scales, automating your development pipeline with **CI/CD** helps manage updates, testing, and deployments efficiently.
   - Automated testing ensures that new features or bug fixes don't break the application, while continuous deployment allows for frequent, reliable releases.

Example:

- A large-scale web application can use Jenkins, GitLab CI, or CircleCI to automate tests and deploy code changes to production without manual intervention, reducing downtime and improving release cycles.

Case Studies of Scalable Python Applications in Real-World Industries

1. **Spotify:**

- o **Challenge**: As a music streaming service with millions of active users, Spotify needed a scalable architecture to handle high volumes of data and requests. They required low latency and real-time recommendations for users.
- o **Solution**: Spotify implemented a microservices architecture using **Python** for certain backend services and leveraged **Apache Kafka** for real-time data streaming. By using containerization with Docker and orchestration via Kubernetes, Spotify can scale individual services independently based on demand.
- o **Result**: Spotify can handle millions of concurrent users and provide real-time personalized music recommendations, all while maintaining high availability and fault tolerance.

2. **Dropbox**:
- o **Challenge**: Dropbox needed to handle large volumes of file storage and synchronization across devices for millions of users. The system had to be highly available, scalable, and capable of processing millions of files efficiently.
- o **Solution**: Dropbox built its file storage system using **Python** for backend services. They use **Amazon S3** for file storage and rely on **Celery** for managing background tasks. They also use

load balancing and **data replication** techniques to ensure high availability and fault tolerance.

- o **Result**: Dropbox's scalable architecture allows it to handle vast amounts of data and millions of file sync requests while maintaining fast response times and reliability.

3. **Instagram**:

- o **Challenge**: As one of the largest social media platforms, Instagram needed a highly scalable system capable of handling millions of photos and videos uploaded daily, alongside interactions such as comments and likes.

- o **Solution**: Instagram relies heavily on **Python** and **Django** for web application development. They use **Cassandra** and **PostgreSQL** for database management and **Redis** for caching. Instagram also uses **load balancing** and **horizontal scaling** to manage traffic spikes.

- o **Result**: Instagram's architecture allows it to handle millions of concurrent users, with a reliable, fast, and highly available system.

Conclusion

Designing scalable Python applications requires a deep understanding of modularity, efficient data management, load balancing, and fault tolerance. By adopting strategies such as microservices, containerization, and event-driven architectures, you can build systems that can grow with your user base and traffic demands. Case studies from companies like Spotify, Dropbox, and Instagram show that Python is capable of handling large-scale systems when designed with scalability in mind. Applying these principles to your own projects will ensure that your applications are both scalable and maintainable, able to handle increasing demands over time.

CHAPTER 10

TESTING, DEBUGGING, AND MAINTAINING PYTHON CODE

Writing clean, maintainable code is only half the battle. Ensuring that code works correctly, identifying issues, and keeping the codebase up to date with minimal risk are essential parts of the development lifecycle. This chapter will dive into how to write robust unit tests, use debugging tools effectively, and implement Continuous Integration (CI) and Continuous Deployment (CD) pipelines to maintain high-quality Python applications.

How to Write Robust Unit Tests with `unittest` *and* `pytest`

1. **Unit Testing with `unittest`:**

    o `unittest` is Python's built-in testing framework. It allows you to write and run unit tests, which are essential for ensuring the correctness of individual units of code.

    o A **unit test** typically tests a small, isolated piece of functionality (like a function or method) to ensure it behaves as expected.

Example of a simple test with `unittest`:

```python
python

import unittest

# Code to be tested
def add(a, b):
    return a + b

class TestAddFunction(unittest.TestCase):
    def test_add_numbers(self):
        self.assertEqual(add(2, 3), 5)   #
Test case to check if add(2, 3) equals 5

    def test_add_negative(self):
        self.assertEqual(add(-1, 1), 0)   #
Test case to check if add(-1, 1) equals 0

if __name__ == '__main__':
    unittest.main()
```

In this example, we define a simple `add` function and test it using two test cases. The `unittest` module offers various assertion methods like `assertEqual`, `assertTrue`, and `assertFalse` to check if the actual output matches the expected output.

2. **Unit Testing with `pytest`:**

    o   `pytest` is a popular third-party testing framework that provides a more flexible and concise syntax than `unittest`. It's especially useful for writing simple tests, handling complex test scenarios, and integrating with other tools.

    o   `pytest` automatically finds and runs tests, and offers advanced features such as fixtures, parameterized tests, and detailed error reporting.

Example of a simple test with `pytest`:

```python
python

# Code to be tested
def multiply(a, b):
    return a * b

# Test functions
def test_multiply_numbers():
    assert multiply(2, 3) == 6

def test_multiply_negative():
    assert multiply(-1, 1) == -1
```

Running the tests is simple: just run `pytest` from the command line, and it will automatically discover the test functions, run them, and report the results.

Advantages of `pytest` over `unittest`:

- ○ Simpler syntax (no need for classes or boilerplate code).
- ○ Automatic test discovery and reporting.
- ○ Advanced features like fixtures, which allow you to set up and tear down test environments efficiently.

3. **Writing Comprehensive Tests**:

- ○ When writing unit tests, make sure to cover a wide range of cases, including:
  - ▪ **Positive test cases**: Testing with valid input.
  - ▪ **Negative test cases**: Testing with invalid input or edge cases (e.g., empty inputs, `None`, etc.).
  - ▪ **Boundary tests**: Testing the limits of input values.

Example:

python

```python
def test_multiply_zero():
    assert multiply(0, 3) == 0  # Boundary
test case
```

Debugging Tools and Techniques in Python

1. **Using the pdb Debugger**:

   o Python's built-in debugger, pdb, allows you to step through your code, inspect variables, and understand how your program is behaving at runtime.

   Example:

```python
import pdb

def add(a, b):
    result = a + b
    pdb.set_trace()  # Set a breakpoint
    return result

add(2, 3)
```

   When the pdb.set_trace() line is executed, the debugger will pause execution, allowing you to interact with the program via the command line. You can use commands like:

   o n: Step to the next line.
   o s: Step into a function.

- o   c: Continue execution.
- o   p: Print the value of a variable (e.g., p result).
- o   q: Quit the debugger.

2. **Logging for Debugging**:
   - o   While pdb is useful for stepping through code, **logging** provides an ongoing record of events in your application. The logging module allows you to add log messages at different levels (e.g., DEBUG, INFO, WARNING, ERROR).

Example:

```python
import logging

logging.basicConfig(level=logging.DEBUG)

def add(a, b):
    logging.debug(f"Adding {a} and {b}")
    return a + b

add(2, 3)
```

The log output will display detailed information about what's happening inside the function, which is particularly useful for debugging in production environments.

106

3. **Third-Party Debugging Tools**:

   o There are also advanced debuggers like **ipdb** (a more interactive version of pdb) and **PyCharm**'s debugger, which provide powerful visual debugging tools for both local and remote debugging.

4. **Error Handling with try, except, and finally**:

   o Proper error handling ensures that your program can gracefully handle unexpected issues, such as invalid input or missing files. The try, except, and finally blocks in Python are used for this purpose.

   Example:

   python

```
try:
    x = int(input("Enter a number: "))
except ValueError:
    print("That's not a valid number!")
finally:
    print("Execution completed.")
```

Continuous Integration (CI) and Continuous Deployment (CD) in Python Applications

1. **What is CI/CD?**

107

- o **Continuous Integration (CI)** involves automatically building and testing code changes as soon as they are committed to the version control system. This ensures that the codebase is always in a working state.

- o **Continuous Deployment (CD)** automates the deployment process, ensuring that code changes are automatically pushed to production after passing tests. This enables rapid, reliable releases.

2. **Setting Up CI/CD with Python**:

- o **GitHub Actions**, **Travis CI**, **CircleCI**, and **GitLab CI/CD** are popular tools for setting up CI/CD pipelines for Python projects.

- o A typical Python CI/CD pipeline consists of the following steps:

    1. **Code Push**: Developer commits code to the repository.

    2. **Build**: CI tool installs dependencies (e.g., using `pip install`).

    3. **Test**: Run unit tests using `pytest` or `unittest` to ensure the code is working.

    4. **Deploy**: If tests pass, the code is automatically deployed to production or staging environments.

3. **Example: GitHub Actions for CI/CD**:

o **Create** a .github/workflows/python-app.yml file for CI/CD:

```yaml
yaml

name: Python application

on: [push]

jobs:
  test:
    runs-on: ubuntu-latest
    steps:
      - name: Check out the repository
        uses: actions/checkout@v2
      - name: Set up Python
        uses: actions/setup-python@v2
        with:
          python-version: 3.8
      - name: Install dependencies
        run: |
          python -m pip install --upgrade pip
          pip install -r requirements.txt
      - name: Run tests
        run: |
          pytest
```

This workflow runs every time code is pushed to the repository. It sets up the Python environment, installs dependencies, and runs tests with `pytest`.

4. **Advantages of CI/CD**:
   o **Faster Development Cycles**: With CI/CD in place, developers can commit changes more frequently, knowing that the system will automatically test and deploy the code.
   o **Reduced Risk**: Automated tests catch bugs early, reducing the risk of introducing errors in production.
   o **Reliable Deployments**: CD ensures that deployments are consistent and automated, reducing human error.

Conclusion

Testing, debugging, and maintaining Python code are vital aspects of the software development lifecycle. By writing robust unit tests using frameworks like `unittest` and `pytest`, you can ensure that your code behaves as expected under various conditions. Debugging tools like `pdb` and logging help you identify and fix issues efficiently. Finally, implementing CI/CD pipelines allows for faster development cycles, consistent deployments, and more reliable software. By integrating these practices into your development workflow, you can ensure that your Python applications are maintainable, bug-free, and ready for production.

CHAPTER 11

WORKING WITH APIS AND WEB FRAMEWORKS

APIs (Application Programming Interfaces) are a crucial component of modern software applications, allowing different systems to communicate with one another. Whether you're building a RESTful API with frameworks like **Flask** or **FastAPI**, or consuming third-party APIs, knowing how to interact with APIs is an essential skill for a Python developer. In this chapter, we'll explore how to build and consume APIs using Python and work with both Flask and FastAPI, two popular frameworks for building web applications. Additionally, we'll look at real-world examples of using APIs to solve common tasks.

Building RESTful APIs with Flask and FastAPI

1. **Building a RESTful API with Flask**:
    o **Flask** is a lightweight, micro web framework for Python. It's well-suited for building simple web applications and APIs. Flask provides flexibility,

allowing you to scale up from small applications to more complex systems.

o To create a RESTful API, Flask uses routes that map HTTP methods (GET, POST, PUT, DELETE) to Python functions.

Example of a simple Flask API:

```python
from flask import Flask, jsonify, request

app = Flask(__name__)

# Sample data
users = [
    {"id": 1, "name": "Alice", "age": 30},
    {"id": 2, "name": "Bob", "age": 25}
]

# Route to fetch all users
@app.route('/users', methods=['GET'])
def get_users():
    return jsonify(users)

# Route to fetch a specific user by ID
@app.route('/users/<int:id>',
methods=['GET'])
def get_user(id):
```

```
    user = next((u for u in users if
u['id'] == id), None)
    if user:
        return jsonify(user)
    return jsonify({"error": "User not
found"}), 404

# Route to add a new user
@app.route('/users', methods=['POST'])
def add_user():
    new_user = request.get_json()
    users.append(new_user)
    return jsonify(new_user), 201

if __name__ == '__main__':
    app.run(debug=True)
```

- **Explanation**:
  - GET /users: Returns a list of all users.
  - GET /users/<id>: Returns the user with the specified id.
  - POST /users: Adds a new user to the list.

Running the Flask API:

- To start the Flask app, run python app.py from the terminal, and the API will be available at http://127.0.0.1:5000.

114

2. **Building a RESTful API with FastAPI**:

   o **FastAPI** is a modern, fast (high-performance) web framework for building APIs with Python. It's built on top of Starlette and Pydantic and is designed for creating RESTful APIs with automatic data validation, serialization, and documentation.

   o FastAPI's main advantage is its high speed, thanks to asynchronous support with `asyncio` and automatic interactive documentation using **Swagger UI**.

   Example of a simple FastAPI API:

```python
from fastapi import FastAPI
from pydantic import BaseModel

app = FastAPI()

# Sample data
users = [
    {"id": 1, "name": "Alice", "age": 30},
    {"id": 2, "name": "Bob", "age": 25}
]

class User(BaseModel):
```

```python
    id: int
    name: str
    age: int

# Route to fetch all users
@app.get("/users")
def get_users():
    return users

# Route to fetch a specific user by ID
@app.get("/users/{id}")
def get_user(id: int):
    user = next((u for u in users if
u['id'] == id), None)
    if user:
        return user
    return {"error": "User not found"}

# Route to add a new user
@app.post("/users")
def add_user(user: User):
    users.append(user.dict())
    return user
```

Explanation:

- o   GET /users: Returns a list of all users.
- o   GET /users/{id}: Returns the user with the specified id.

o   `POST` `/users`: Adds a new user by accepting a `User` object.

Running the FastAPI app:

o   To start the FastAPI app, run `uvicorn app:app --reload`, and the API will be available at `http://127.0.0.1:8000`.

FastAPI also generates interactive documentation, accessible at `http://127.0.0.1:8000/docs`.

Working with Third-Party APIs Using Python

1. **Making HTTP Requests with `requests`:**
    o   The **requests** library is one of the most popular Python libraries for making HTTP requests. It abstracts away the complexity of sending HTTP requests, allowing you to easily interact with third-party APIs.

    Example of consuming a third-party API (getting weather data from OpenWeatherMap API):

```python
python

import requests
```

```python
api_key = "your_api_key"
city = "London"
url                                    =
f"http://api.openweathermap.org/data/2.5/
weather?q={city}&appid={api_key}"

response = requests.get(url)
data = response.json()

if response.status_code == 200:
    print(f"Weather        in        {city}:
{data['weather'][0]['description']}")
else:
    print(f"Error        fetching        data:
{data['message']}")
```

Explanation:

- o The script fetches weather information for the specified `city` using the OpenWeatherMap API. The `requests.get()` function sends an HTTP GET request, and the `response.json()` method parses the JSON data returned by the API.

2. **Working with OAuth Authentication**:

- o Many APIs require OAuth authentication to access user data securely. The **requests-**

oauthlib library can be used to interact with OAuth-protected APIs.

Example (using OAuth2 with GitHub API):

python

```
from        requests_oauthlib        import
OAuth2Session
from        oauthlib.oauth2        import
WebApplicationClient

client_id = 'your_client_id'
client_secret = 'your_client_secret'
authorization_base_url                    =
'https://github.com/login/oauth/authorize
'
token_url                                 =
'https://github.com/login/oauth/access_to
ken'

client = WebApplicationClient(client_id)

# Step 1: Get authorization code
oauth       =        OAuth2Session(client_id,
redirect_uri='http://localhost/callback')
authorization_url,        state        =
oauth.authorization_url(authorization_bas
e_url)
```

```
print('Please    go    to    %s    and    authorize
access.' % authorization_url)

# Step   2:   Get   the   token   using   the
authorization code
redirect_response = input('Paste the full
redirect URL here: ')
oauth.fetch_token(token_url,
authorization_response=redirect_response,

client_secret=client_secret)

# Step   3:   Use   the   token   to   make
authenticated API requests
response                                   =
oauth.get('https://api.github.com/user')
print(response.json())
```

Explanation:

- o This example shows how to authenticate with GitHub's OAuth2 system and retrieve user data once authorized.

Real-World Examples of Creating and Consuming APIs

1. **Creating an API for a Todo Application**:

o Imagine you're building a simple Todo application where users can add, update, and delete tasks. Using **FastAPI** or **Flask**, you can create a RESTful API that interacts with a database (e.g., SQLite, PostgreSQL) to manage tasks.

o Endpoints might include:

- `GET /todos`: Retrieve a list of tasks.

- `POST /todos`: Add a new task.

- `PUT /todos/{id}`: Update an existing task.

- `DELETE /todos/{id}`: Delete a task.

2. **Consuming a Social Media API (Twitter API)**:

o You might want to retrieve the latest tweets from a user's timeline using Twitter's REST API. Using **requests** or **requests-oauthlib**, you can send authenticated API requests to retrieve tweets and analyze sentiment or display them in your application.

Example (fetching tweets):

```python
python

import requests
from requests_oauthlib import OAuth1
```

```
auth        =        OAuth1('consumer_key',
'consumer_secret',        'access_token',
'access_token_secret')
url = 'https://api.twitter.com/2/tweets'

response = requests.get(url, auth=auth)
print(response.json())
```

3. **Building an API for an E-commerce Site**:

   o An e-commerce platform might expose APIs for product catalog, user authentication, shopping cart management, and order processing.

   o **FastAPI** or **Flask** can be used to build these APIs, with endpoints like:

     ▪ GET /products: Fetch the list of products.

     ▪ POST /orders: Create a new order.

     ▪ PUT /orders/{id}: Update the status of an order.

     ▪ DELETE /orders/{id}: Cancel an order.

Conclusion

APIs are at the core of modern software development, allowing different applications and systems to communicate. Whether you are building a RESTful API with **Flask** or

FastAPI or consuming third-party APIs with **requests** or **OAuth**, Python offers powerful libraries and frameworks to simplify these tasks. In real-world applications, APIs enable you to create scalable and flexible systems, whether it's an e-commerce platform, a social media app, or a weather service. By mastering the creation and consumption of APIs, you can build robust, interactive, and dynamic applications.

CHAPTER 12

MACHINE LEARNING AND DATA SCIENCE IN PYTHON

Python has become the go-to language for data analysis, machine learning (ML), and data science due to its simplicity and rich ecosystem of libraries. In this chapter, we'll explore how to use Python for data analysis with popular libraries like **pandas** and **NumPy**, introduce machine learning concepts with **scikit-learn** and **TensorFlow**, and walk through building a simple machine learning model with real-world data.

Using Python for Data Analysis with Libraries like pandas and NumPy

1. **pandas**:
   - **pandas** is a powerful Python library used for data manipulation and analysis. It provides data structures like **DataFrame** and **Series**, which are efficient for handling and analyzing structured data (like tables and spreadsheets).

- o Common operations in **pandas** include data loading, cleaning, aggregation, and transformation.

Example of using pandas:

```python

import pandas as pd

# Loading a CSV file into a DataFrame
data = pd.read_csv('data.csv')

# Displaying the first 5 rows of the data
print(data.head())

# Cleaning data: Remove rows with missing values
data = data.dropna()

# Grouping data by a column and calculating the mean
grouped_data = data.groupby('Category')['Value'].mean()
print(grouped_data)
```

Common pandas operations:

- o **Filtering**: `data[data['column_name'] > value]`
- o **Sorting**:
  `data.sort_values(by='column_name')`
- o **Aggregating**:
  `data.groupby('category').agg('mean')`
- o **Merging**: `pd.merge(df1, df2, on='key_column')`

2. **NumPy**:

- o **NumPy** is a fundamental library for numerical computations in Python. It provides support for arrays and matrices, as well as a large collection of mathematical functions to operate on these arrays.
- o **NumPy** is especially useful when performing mathematical and statistical operations on data.

Example of using NumPy:

```python
import numpy as np

# Creating a NumPy array
arr = np.array([1, 2, 3, 4, 5])

# Performing basic operations
```

```
print(arr + 10)  # Adding 10 to each element
print(np.mean(arr))  # Calculating the mean
print(np.std(arr))    #  Calculating  the
standard deviation
```

Common NumPy operations:

- o **Array   creation**:   np.array(),
  np.linspace(),np.zeros()
- o **Mathematical   operations**:   np.add(),
  np.mean(),np.dot()
- o **Array   manipulation**:   np.reshape(),
  np.transpose(),np.concatenate()

Introduction to Machine Learning Concepts with scikit-learn and TensorFlow

1. **scikit-learn**:
   - o **scikit-learn** is a simple and efficient machine learning library for Python. It provides tools for data mining, machine learning algorithms, and model evaluation. It's ideal for beginners and intermediate developers.
   - o Common machine learning tasks with scikit-learn include classification, regression, clustering, and dimensionality reduction.

Example of building a simple model with scikit-learn:

python

```python
from sklearn.model_selection import train_test_split
from sklearn.ensemble import RandomForestClassifier
from sklearn.metrics import accuracy_score

# Example dataset: Iris dataset (available in scikit-learn)
from sklearn.datasets import load_iris
iris = load_iris()
X = iris.data
y = iris.target

# Splitting data into training and testing sets
X_train, X_test, y_train, y_test = train_test_split(X, y, test_size=0.2)

# Building and training the model
model = RandomForestClassifier()
model.fit(X_train, y_train)

# Making predictions and evaluating the model
```

```
y_pred = model.predict(X_test)
print(f"Accuracy: {accuracy_score(y_test,
y_pred)}")
```

Key scikit-learn tools:

- o **Models**: RandomForestClassifier, LinearRegression, KMeans, etc.
- o **Preprocessing**: StandardScaler, LabelEncoder, OneHotEncoder
- o **Model evaluation**: accuracy_score, confusion_matrix, cross_val_score

2. **TensorFlow**:

- o **TensorFlow** is an open-source machine learning framework primarily used for deep learning applications. It allows you to build and train complex neural networks for tasks like image recognition, natural language processing (NLP), and reinforcement learning.
- o TensorFlow is highly scalable, supports GPU acceleration, and provides APIs for both beginners and advanced users.

Example of building a simple neural network with TensorFlow:

```
python
```

129

```python
import tensorflow as tf
from tensorflow.keras.models import Sequential
from tensorflow.keras.layers import Dense
from sklearn.datasets import load_iris
from sklearn.model_selection import train_test_split

# Load the dataset
iris = load_iris()
X = iris.data
y = iris.target

# Split data into training and testing sets
X_train, X_test, y_train, y_test = train_test_split(X, y, test_size=0.2)

# Build a simple neural network model
model = Sequential([
    Dense(10, activation='relu', input_shape=(X.shape[1],)),
    Dense(3, activation='softmax')   # 3 output neurons for 3 classes
])

# Compile the model
```

```
model.compile(optimizer='adam',
loss='sparse_categorical_crossentropy',
metrics=['accuracy'])

# Train the model
model.fit(X_train, y_train, epochs=50)

# Evaluate the model
loss, accuracy = model.evaluate(X_test,
y_test)
print(f"Accuracy: {accuracy}")
```

Key TensorFlow concepts:

- o **Tensors**: Multidimensional arrays used in TensorFlow for data representation.
- o **Keras**: A high-level API for building neural networks in TensorFlow.
- o **Layers**: Building blocks for creating neural networks (e.g., `Dense`, `Conv2D`).
- o **Training**: Using `fit()`, `compile()`, and `evaluate()` to train and assess models.

Building a Simple Machine Learning Model in Python with Real-World Data

Let's walk through a real-world example where we build a simple machine learning model using scikit-learn to predict housing prices based on features like the number of rooms, location, and property type. We will use the **Boston Housing Dataset**, which is commonly used for regression tasks.

1. **Dataset**:
   - The **Boston Housing Dataset** contains features like average number of rooms, crime rate, distance to employment centers, and more, used to predict the median value of homes in Boston.

2. **Steps**:
1.   Load the dataset.
   2. Split the data into training and testing sets.
   3. Build a regression model.
   4. Train and evaluate the model.

Example:

python

```python
from sklearn.datasets import load_boston
from sklearn.model_selection import train_test_split
from sklearn.linear_model import LinearRegression
from sklearn.metrics import mean_squared_error

# Load the Boston housing dataset
```

```python
boston = load_boston()
X = boston.data
y = boston.target

# Split the data into training and testing
sets
X_train, X_test, y_train, y_test =
train_test_split(X, y, test_size=0.2,
random_state=42)

# Build the linear regression model
model = LinearRegression()

# Train the model
model.fit(X_train, y_train)

# Make predictions
y_pred = model.predict(X_test)

# Evaluate the model
mse = mean_squared_error(y_test, y_pred)
print(f"Mean Squared Error: {mse}")
```

In this example:

- o We use the **LinearRegression** model to predict housing prices.
- o **Mean Squared Error (MSE)** is used to evaluate how well our model predicts the prices.

3. **Model Improvements**:

   o You can improve the model by performing feature engineering, normalizing the data, and trying different algorithms (e.g., **RandomForestRegressor, SVR**).

   o Hyperparameter tuning using **GridSearchCV** or **RandomizedSearchCV** can help optimize the model further.

Conclusion

In this chapter, we've explored the foundations of **data analysis** and **machine learning** in Python using **pandas** and **NumPy** for data manipulation, and **scikit-learn** and **TensorFlow** for building machine learning models. We built a simple regression model to predict housing prices, using real-world data. Understanding how to preprocess, analyze, and model data with these powerful libraries is essential for solving complex problems in data science and machine learning.

By continuing to explore these libraries and techniques, you can build more sophisticated models and apply them to real-world datasets across a wide range of industries, from finance and healthcare to e-commerce and entertainment.

CHAPTER 13

SECURITY BEST PRACTICES FOR PYTHON DEVELOPERS

As Python developers, ensuring the security of your applications is essential to prevent unauthorized access, data breaches, and vulnerabilities. This chapter will cover common security vulnerabilities and how to avoid them, techniques for securing web applications, handling sensitive data, and implementing user authentication. We'll also explore real-world examples of security practices in Python applications.

Overview of Common Security Vulnerabilities and How to Avoid Them

1. **SQL Injection**:

    o **What it is**: SQL Injection occurs when an attacker inserts malicious SQL code into a query, allowing them to manipulate the database or retrieve sensitive information.

    o **How to avoid it**:

- Use **parameterized queries** or **prepared statements** instead of string concatenation.
- **ORMs** like **SQLAlchemy** automatically protect against SQL injection by escaping parameters in queries.

Example:

python

```
# Vulnerable code (do not use!)
cursor.execute(f"SELECT * FROM users WHERE
username = '{username}' AND password =
'{password}'")

# Safe code using parameterized queries
(using SQLAlchemy or cursor.execute)
cursor.execute("SELECT * FROM users WHERE
username = %s AND password = %s",
(username, password))
```

2. **Cross-Site Scripting (XSS)**:
   - **What it is**: XSS vulnerabilities occur when an attacker injects malicious scripts into web pages viewed by other users. This can lead to data theft or unauthorized actions.
   - **How to avoid it**:

- Always **escape user input** and sanitize any data that's inserted into web pages.
- Use libraries like **Jinja2** (in Flask) to automatically escape variables in templates.

Example:

```html
html

<!-- Potential XSS vulnerability -->
<div>{{ user_input }}</div>

<!-- Safe usage with Flask/Jinja2 -->
<div>{{ user_input|e }}</div>  <!-- The 'e'
filter escapes special characters -->
```

3. **Cross-Site Request Forgery (CSRF)**:

   o **What it is**: CSRF is an attack where a malicious user tricks the victim into performing actions on a website without their consent, often leading to unauthorized actions like changing account settings or making transactions.

   o **How to avoid it**:

      - Use **anti-CSRF tokens** to ensure that requests originate from the authenticated user.

- Most modern frameworks (like **Flask** and **Django**) include CSRF protection middleware by default.

Example in Flask:

```python

from flask_wtf.csrf import CSRFProtect

app = Flask(__name__)
csrf = CSRFProtect(app)

@app.route('/submit', methods=['POST'])
def submit_form():
    # CSRF token will automatically be validated
    pass
```

4. **Insecure Deserialization**:
   - **What it is**: Insecure deserialization occurs when untrusted data is deserialized into objects, potentially allowing attackers to execute arbitrary code.
   - **How to avoid it**:
     - **Never deserialize** data from untrusted sources without proper validation.

- Use **JSON** or **XML** formats instead of Python's `pickle` module, which can be insecure when handling user input.

Example:

```python
python

# Avoid using pickle for untrusted data
import pickle
# Dangerous! Do not use pickle.load() with untrusted data.
user_data = pickle.load(request.data)

# Instead, use JSON (safe)
import json
user_data = json.loads(request.data)
```

Techniques for Securing Web Applications, Handling Sensitive Data, and User Authentication

1. **Securing Web Applications**:
   o **HTTPS**: Always use **HTTPS** (HyperText Transfer Protocol Secure) to encrypt data between the client and the server.
      - Use **SSL/TLS certificates** (can be obtained through **Let's Encrypt** for free) to ensure encrypted communication.

- Redirect all HTTP traffic to HTTPS to prevent man-in-the-middle attacks.

Example (Flask):

```python
python

from flask import Flask, redirect, request

app = Flask(__name__)

@app.before_request
def before_request():
    if request.is_secure is False:
        return
redirect(request.url.replace("http://",
"https://"))
```

2. **Handling Sensitive Data**:
   - o **Encryption**: Store sensitive information like passwords or personal data in an encrypted format.
   - o Use libraries like **cryptography** to securely encrypt and decrypt data.

Example (Password hashing with bcrypt):

```python
python
```

```
import bcrypt

# Hashing a password
password = b"super_secret_password"
hashed_password = bcrypt.hashpw(password,
bcrypt.gensalt())

# Verifying a password
if              bcrypt.checkpw(password,
hashed_password):
    print("Password match!")
else:
    print("Incorrect password.")
```

o **Sensitive Data Handling**: Avoid storing sensitive data like plain-text passwords, API keys, or financial information. Always store these securely and minimize their exposure.

Example (Environment variables for API keys):

```
python

import os

API_KEY = os.getenv('API_KEY')   # Store
sensitive keys in environment variables
```

3. **User Authentication**:

- o **Session Management**: Use **secure cookies** to manage user sessions. Set the `HttpOnly` and `Secure` flags on cookies to prevent unauthorized access and interception.
- o **OAuth2**: Use OAuth2 for secure user authentication, especially when dealing with third-party services (e.g., Google, Facebook).

Example (OAuth2 Authentication with `requests-oauthlib`):

python

```
from         requests_oauthlib         import
OAuth2Session

# OAuth2 for Google login
client_id = 'your-client-id'
client_secret = 'your-client-secret'
authorization_base_url                    =
'https://accounts.google.com/o/oauth2/aut
h'
token_url                                  =
'https://accounts.google.com/o/oauth2/tok
en'

oauth = OAuth2Session(client_id)
```

```
authorization_url,          state          =
oauth.authorization_url(authorization_bas
e_url)

print('Please  go  to  %s  and  authorize
access.' % authorization_url)

redirect_response = input('Paste the full
redirect URL here: ')
oauth.fetch_token(token_url,
authorization_response=redirect_response,
client_secret=client_secret)

# Make an authenticated request
response                               =
oauth.get('https://www.googleapis.com/oau
th2/v1/userinfo')
print(response.json())
```

- o Use **multi-factor authentication (MFA)** to add an extra layer of security for sensitive user actions.

4. **Logging and Monitoring**:
   - o Implement logging to track security-related events (e.g., login attempts, access to sensitive data).

o Monitor logs for suspicious activities and potential attacks (like brute-force attempts or SQL injection).

Example (Logging in Python):

```python
import logging

logging.basicConfig(level=logging.INFO)
logger = logging.getLogger(__name__)

logger.info("User logged in successfully")
logger.error("Failed login attempt")
```

Real-World Examples of Security Implementations in Python Apps

1. **Flask Application with User Authentication**:
   o A Flask application with user authentication, where passwords are hashed using **bcrypt** and sessions are managed securely using **Flask-Login**.

Example:

```python
from flask import Flask, render_template,
redirect, url_for, request, session
```

```python
from flask_bcrypt import Bcrypt
from flask_login import LoginManager,
UserMixin, login_user, login_required,
logout_user

app = Flask(__name__)
app.secret_key = 'your_secret_key'
bcrypt = Bcrypt(app)
login_manager = LoginManager(app)

# User model
class User(UserMixin):
    def __init__(self, id, username,
password_hash):
        self.id = id
        self.username = username
        self.password_hash = password_hash

users_db = {"user1": User(1, "user1",
bcrypt.generate_password_hash("password12
3").decode('utf-8'))}

@app.route('/login',        methods=['GET',
'POST'])
def login():
    if request.method == 'POST':
        username                          =
request.form['username']
```

```
        password                    =
request.form['password']
        user = users_db.get(username)
        if           user           and
bcrypt.check_password_hash(user.password_
hash, password):
            login_user(user)
            return
redirect(url_for('dashboard'))
        return "Invalid credentials", 401
    return render_template('login.html')


@app.route('/dashboard')
@login_required
def dashboard():
    return "Welcome to your dashboard!"


@app.route('/logout')
def logout():
    logout_user()
    return redirect(url_for('login'))


if __name__ == '__main__':
    app.run(debug=True)
```

2. Securing API Endpoints with Flask-JWT:

- o Securing RESTful API endpoints using JSON Web Tokens (JWT) for user authentication and ensuring only authorized users can access the resources.

Example:

python

```
import jwt
from datetime import datetime, timedelta
from flask import Flask, request, jsonify

app = Flask(__name__)
SECRET_KEY = 'your_secret_key'

def create_token(user_id):
    expiration = datetime.utcnow() + timedelta(hours=1)
    payload = {'user_id': user_id, 'exp': expiration}
    return jwt.encode(payload, SECRET_KEY, algorithm='HS256')

@app.route('/login', methods=['POST'])
def login():
    username = request.json.get('username')
    password = request.json.get('password')
```

```
        if username == 'admin' and password ==
'admin123':
            token = create_token(user_id=1)
            return jsonify({"token": token})
        return 'Unauthorized', 401


@app.route('/protected', methods=['GET'])
def protected():
    token                                  =
request.headers.get('Authorization')
    if not token:
        return 'Token is missing', 403
    try:
        payload    =    jwt.decode(token,
SECRET_KEY, algorithms=['HS256'])
        return jsonify({"message": "Access
granted"})
    except jwt.ExpiredSignatureError:
        return 'Token expired', 401
    except jwt.InvalidTokenError:
        return 'Invalid token', 401


if __name__ == '__main__':
    app.run(debug=True)
```

Conclusion

Securing your Python applications is essential to protect sensitive data and prevent common attacks. By implementing best practices like input validation, encryption, secure authentication, and logging, you can create robust applications that withstand common security vulnerabilities. Incorporating **Flask** and **FastAPI** for secure web applications, using **OAuth** for user authentication, and following general security guidelines will help ensure that your Python applications are both secure and maintainable.

CHAPTER 14

PYTHON FOR CLOUD DEVELOPMENT

Cloud development has transformed how applications are built, deployed, and scaled. With the help of platforms like **AWS**, **Azure**, and **Google Cloud**, developers can create cloud-native applications that are scalable, resilient, and cost-efficient. In this chapter, we'll explore how to develop cloud-native applications with Python, automate deployment, and scale applications using cloud platforms. We will also look at real-world examples of cloud applications built with Python.

How to Develop Cloud-Native Applications with Python (AWS, Azure, Google Cloud)

1. **Cloud-Native Applications**:

    o   A cloud-native application is designed to fully exploit the benefits of cloud platforms. These applications are built with microservices, containers, and are designed to be scalable, fault-tolerant, and flexible.

o   Python, with its wide array of libraries and frameworks, is an ideal language for building cloud-native applications that run efficiently in distributed environments.

2. **Using Python with AWS**:

o   **Amazon Web Services (AWS)** is one of the most widely used cloud platforms for building, deploying, and managing applications. AWS provides a variety of services, including compute power (EC2), storage (S3), and databases (RDS, DynamoDB).

Example: Building a Simple AWS Lambda Function with Python:

o   **AWS Lambda** allows you to run code without provisioning or managing servers. You upload your Python function, and AWS Lambda automatically scales the function to handle incoming requests.

Steps:

o   Create an AWS Lambda function.

o   Configure the Lambda function to be triggered by an AWS service like S3 or API Gateway.

Lambda function example:

```python
python

import json

def lambda_handler(event, context):
    # Your function logic here
    name = event.get('name', 'World')
    return {
        'statusCode': 200,
        'body':         json.dumps(f'Hello,
{name}!')
    }
```

- o You can deploy this Lambda function through the AWS Console or use the **AWS CLI** or **AWS SDK for Python (Boto3)** to automate the deployment.

Using Boto3 to interact with AWS:

```python
python

import boto3

# Create an S3 client
s3 = boto3.client('s3')
```

```
# List all buckets in S3
response = s3.list_buckets()
for bucket in response['Buckets']:
    print(f'Bucket                 Name:
{bucket["Name"]}')
```

3. **Using Python with Azure**:

   o **Microsoft Azure** provides a robust cloud environment for building and deploying applications, with support for Python through various services like **Azure App Services**, **Azure Functions**, and **Azure Kubernetes Service (AKS)**.

Example: Deploying a Python Web App to Azure App Service:

   o **Azure App Service** provides a fully managed platform for building and hosting web applications. You can use **Flask**, **Django**, or **FastAPI** to develop your web app and then deploy it to Azure.

Steps:

   o Create a **Python Web App** in Azure.
   o Push your code to Azure using GitHub or Azure DevOps.

153

Flask app example:

```python
python

from flask import Flask

app = Flask(__name__)

@app.route('/')
def hello_world():
    return 'Hello, Azure!'

if __name__ == '__main__':
    app.run(debug=True)
```

To deploy this application:

- o   Create a web app in Azure using the Azure portal.
- o   Use the **Azure CLI** to deploy your Flask application to the cloud.

4. **Using Python with Google Cloud**:
    - o   **Google Cloud Platform (GCP)** provides various services for Python development, including **Google App Engine**, **Google Kubernetes Engine (GKE)**, and **Cloud Functions**.

    Example: Deploying a Python Application to Google App Engine:

o **Google App Engine** is a platform for building and deploying applications without managing the underlying infrastructure. You can deploy Python web applications using **Flask** or **FastAPI**.

Steps:

o Install the **Google Cloud SDK**.
o Create a simple Python app using Flask.

Flask app example:

```python
from flask import Flask

app = Flask(__name__)

@app.route('/')
def hello_world():
    return 'Hello, Google Cloud!'

if __name__ == '__main__':
    app.run(debug=True)
```

To deploy this app:

o Create a `app.yaml` configuration file for Google App Engine:

155

```yaml
yaml

runtime: python39
entrypoint: gunicorn -b :$PORT main:app
```

- o Use the `gcloud` command to deploy the application:

```bash
bash

gcloud app deploy
```

Once deployed, your application will be accessible via a URL provided by Google Cloud.

Automating Deployment and Scaling Applications Using Cloud Platforms

1. **Automating Deployment**:
   - o Cloud platforms provide various ways to automate the deployment process. This can be done using **CI/CD pipelines**, **serverless functions**, or **Kubernetes** for container orchestration.

   Example: Using GitHub Actions for Continuous Deployment:

o With **GitHub Actions**, you can automate the deployment of your Python application to AWS, Azure, or Google Cloud.

o Below is an example of a GitHub Actions workflow to deploy a Flask application to **AWS Elastic Beanstalk**:

```yaml
name: Deploy to Elastic Beanstalk

on:
  push:
    branches:
      - main

jobs:
  deploy:
    runs-on: ubuntu-latest
    steps:
      - name: Checkout code
        uses: actions/checkout@v2

      - name: Set up Python
        uses: actions/setup-python@v2
        with:
          python-version: '3.x'

      - name: Install dependencies
```

```
run: |
    python -m pip install --upgrade
pip
    pip install -r requirements.txt


- name: Deploy to Elastic Beanstalk
  run: |
      eb init -p python-3.x --region
us-west-2
      eb deploy
  env:
      AWS_ACCESS_KEY_ID:          ${{
secrets.AWS_ACCESS_KEY_ID }}
      AWS_SECRET_ACCESS_KEY:      ${{
secrets.AWS_SECRET_ACCESS_KEY }}
```

2. **Scaling Applications**:

    o **Horizontal scaling**: This involves adding more
       instances of your application to handle increased
       traffic. Cloud platforms like AWS, Azure, and
       Google Cloud provide auto-scaling features.

    o **Vertical scaling**: This involves increasing the
       resources (CPU, memory) available to a single
       instance. Cloud platforms allow you to adjust the
       instance size based on your app's demands.

Example: Auto-scaling with AWS EC2:

o   AWS **Auto Scaling** automatically adjusts the number of EC2 instances running your application based on demand. You can define policies for scaling in/out based on metrics like CPU utilization or network traffic.

Real-World Examples of Cloud Applications Built with Python

1. **Serverless Functions with AWS Lambda**:
    o   **Scenario**: You need to process images uploaded to an S3 bucket and generate thumbnails.
    o   **Solution**: Create an AWS Lambda function in Python that is triggered by S3 events (when a new image is uploaded). The Lambda function resizes the image and stores the thumbnail in another S3 bucket.

Example Lambda Function:

```python
import boto3
from PIL import Image
from io import BytesIO

s3 = boto3.client('s3')

def lambda_handler(event, context):
```

```
    bucket                              =
event['Records'][0]['s3']['bucket']['name
']
    key                                 =
event['Records'][0]['s3']['object']['key'
]

    # Fetch the image from S3
    response                            =
s3.get_object(Bucket=bucket, Key=key)
    img = Image.open(response['Body'])

    # Generate thumbnail
    img.thumbnail((128, 128))

    # Save the thumbnail to another bucket
    thumb_buffer = BytesIO()
    img.save(thumb_buffer, 'JPEG')
    thumb_buffer.seek(0)
    s3.put_object(Bucket='your-thumbnail-
bucket', Key=key, Body=thumb_buffer)
    return {'statusCode': 200, 'body':
'Thumbnail generated'}
```

2. **Building a Scalable Web Application with Flask on Google Cloud**:

   o **Scenario**: You need to build a web application that scales dynamically with traffic and stores data in **Google Cloud SQL** (MySQL).

160

o **Solution**: Deploy the Flask app to **Google App Engine** (with auto-scaling enabled) and connect it to **Cloud SQL** to manage user data.

Example Flask app with Cloud SQL:

```python
from flask import Flask, request
import mysql.connector

app = Flask(__name__)

@app.route('/')
def index():
    conn = mysql.connector.connect(
        user='root',
        password='your_password',
        host='127.0.0.1', database='mydatabase')
    cursor = conn.cursor()
    cursor.execute('SELECT * FROM users')
    users = cursor.fetchall()
    conn.close()
    return str(users)

if __name__ == '__main__':
    app.run(debug=True)
```

Deploy this app to Google App Engine, and it will automatically scale based on traffic.

Conclusion

Developing cloud-native applications with Python allows you to leverage the flexibility and scalability of cloud platforms like AWS, Azure, and Google Cloud. By using tools like **AWS Lambda**, **Google App Engine**, **Azure Functions**, and automating deployment with CI/CD pipelines, you can quickly scale your applications to meet growing demand. Real-world examples of serverless functions, scalable web apps, and automated deployments demonstrate how Python can be integrated with the cloud to build powerful, efficient applications.

CHAPTER 15

MODERN PYTHON FRAMEWORKS AND LIBRARIES

Python has become one of the most versatile programming languages, thanks to a rich ecosystem of frameworks and libraries that make development faster, easier, and more efficient. In this chapter, we'll explore some of the most popular Python frameworks and libraries used in modern development, including **Django**, **Flask**, **FastAPI**, and **Pydantic**. We'll also discuss how to choose the right framework for your project and provide real-world examples of how these tools are used in building Python applications.

Overview of Popular Python Frameworks and Libraries for Modern Development

1. **Django**:
   - o **Django** is a high-level Python web framework that promotes rapid development and clean, pragmatic design. It follows the **Model-View-Template (MVT)** architectural pattern and includes many built-in features for web

development, such as authentication, form handling, and an admin interface.

- o Django is best suited for projects that require a lot of built-in functionality and need to scale quickly, such as content management systems (CMS), e-commerce websites, and social platforms.

Key features:

- o **Built-in ORM** (Object-Relational Mapping) for database management.
- o **Admin panel**: Automatically generated and customizable for managing data.
- o **Security**: Built-in protection against common security threats like SQL injection, XSS, and CSRF.
- o **Scalability**: Suitable for both small and large-scale applications.

Example: Django Web App Setup:

```bash

pip install django
django-admin startproject myproject
cd myproject
python manage.py startapp myapp
```

Once the app is set up, you can start adding views, models, and templates for dynamic content generation.

2. **Flask**:

   o **Flask** is a lightweight web framework for Python that provides the bare essentials for building web applications. It's simple, flexible, and allows you to add only the components you need.

   o Flask is ideal for smaller projects or applications that require fine-grained control over the components and do not require the full suite of features that Django offers.

Key features:

   o **Minimalistic**: Flask provides the essentials but leaves the rest to the developer.

   o **Flexible**: You can choose your database, template engine, and third-party libraries.

   o **Extensible**: Easily extendable with third-party extensions for added functionality like authentication, database integration, etc.

Example: Flask Web App Setup:

```bash
```

```
pip install flask
python

from flask import Flask

app = Flask(__name__)

@app.route('/')
def home():
    return "Hello, Flask!"

if __name__ == '__main__':
    app.run(debug=True)
```

Flask provides full flexibility, allowing you to build small-scale applications or APIs with ease.

3. **FastAPI**:
   - o **FastAPI** is a modern, high-performance web framework for building APIs. It is based on Python type hints and uses asynchronous programming to deliver high speed and scalability.
   - o FastAPI is designed for building **RESTful APIs** and is often used when performance is crucial (e.g., in microservices or high-load applications).

Key features:

- o **Asynchronous**: Supports `async` and `await` for non-blocking operations.
- o **Automatic validation**: Uses **Pydantic** for data validation and serialization.
- o **Automatic API documentation**: Built-in integration with **Swagger UI** and **ReDoc** for API docs.

Example: FastAPI Web App Setup:

```bash
pip install fastapi uvicorn
python
```

```python
from fastapi import FastAPI

app = FastAPI()

@app.get("/")
def read_root():
    return {"message": "Hello, FastAPI"}

if __name__ == '__main__':
    import uvicorn
    uvicorn.run(app,      host="127.0.0.1",
port=8000)
```

FastAPI's automatic API documentation and high performance make it an ideal choice for building efficient and scalable APIs.

4. **Pydantic**:

    o   **Pydantic** is a data validation library that is used in conjunction with FastAPI but can also be used independently. It uses Python type annotations to enforce data validation, making it easier to define, parse, and validate data.

    o   Pydantic is especially useful when building APIs or handling structured data in Python.

    Key features:

    o   **Type safety**: Uses Python's type hints for data validation.

    o   **Data serialization**: Easily convert between Python objects and data formats (e.g., JSON).

    o   **Error handling**: Automatically raises detailed validation errors when data doesn't meet the expected format.

    Example: Using Pydantic for Data Validation:

    ```python
    python
    ```

```python
from pydantic import BaseModel

class User(BaseModel):
    name: str
    age: int

user = User(name="Alice", age=30)
print(user.dict())    # {'name': 'Alice', 'age': 30}

# This will raise a validation error
because the age is not an integer
#    user    =    User(name="Bob", age="not_a_number")
```

Pydantic allows you to handle and validate structured data efficiently, and it integrates well with FastAPI for API development.

Choosing the Right Framework for Your Project

When choosing a framework, you should consider the following factors:

1. **Project Size and Complexity**:
   - o   If you are building a **large-scale application** with many built-in features (e.g., authentication, database management, and an admin panel),

Django is a great choice due to its comprehensive feature set.

- o For **smaller applications** or APIs where flexibility and simplicity are key, **Flask** is ideal because of its lightweight, modular approach.
- o If your primary goal is to build **high-performance RESTful APIs**, then **FastAPI** is the best option, thanks to its asynchronous capabilities and automatic validation.

2. **Performance**:
   - o **FastAPI** is the fastest framework for APIs, especially when dealing with high concurrency and real-time processing.
   - o **Flask** and **Django** are great choices, but FastAPI's support for async tasks gives it an edge for performance-critical applications.

3. **Ease of Use**:
   - o **Flask** is the most straightforward framework, with minimal setup and clear documentation, making it a great choice for beginners or smaller projects.
   - o **Django** comes with more features out-of-the-box but can be more complex to configure and learn.

4. **Development Speed**:

o If you need to rapidly prototype and need built-in tools (e.g., admin panel, authentication), **Django** is the most suitable framework.

o **Flask** gives you more control and flexibility, while **FastAPI** speeds up the development of APIs by providing automatic validation and documentation.

Real-World Examples of Using Modern Frameworks to Build Python Applications

1. **Building an E-Commerce Platform with Django**:

   o A real-world application where Django can be used to build a scalable e-commerce website. Django's built-in **admin panel** makes it easy for administrators to manage products, users, and orders.

   o **Integration with payment gateways** (e.g., Stripe, PayPal) for secure payment processing.

Example Django features for E-commerce:

   o **User authentication** for account management.

   o **Product catalog management** with an easy-to-use interface for adding and updating products.

   o **Order management** for tracking and processing customer orders.

2. **Building a Real-Time Chat Application with Flask and WebSockets**:

   o Flask, along with **Flask-SocketIO**, can be used to build a real-time chat application. This allows users to send messages in real-time, using WebSockets for bidirectional communication.

   o **Flask-SocketIO** allows for event-driven communication and asynchronous processing, making it suitable for real-time apps.

Example Flask code for WebSockets:

python

```python
from flask import Flask, render_template
from flask_socketio import SocketIO, send

app = Flask(__name__)
socketio = SocketIO(app)

@app.route('/')
def index():
    return render_template('chat.html')

@socketio.on('message')
def handle_message(msg):
    send(msg, broadcast=True)
```

```
if __name__ == '__main__':
    socketio.run(app)
```

3. **Building a High-Performance API with FastAPI**:

   o FastAPI is ideal for building APIs that need to handle many requests per second, such as microservices, data processing APIs, or real-time analytics APIs.

   o **Integration with databases** using **SQLAlchemy** and **Pydantic** for input validation.

Example FastAPI API:

python

```python
from fastapi import FastAPI
from pydantic import BaseModel

app = FastAPI()

class Item(BaseModel):
    name: str
    price: float

@app.post("/items/")
async def create_item(item: Item):
    return {"name": item.name, "price": item.price}
```

FastAPI allows you to create a fast, asynchronous API with minimal effort and integrates well with **SQLAlchemy** and **Pydantic** for backend management and validation.

Conclusion

In this chapter, we have explored popular Python frameworks such as **Django, Flask, FastAPI**, and **Pydantic**, each of which is well-suited to different types of projects. Choosing the right framework depends on your specific needs, whether it's rapid development, flexibility, performance, or scalability. By understanding these tools and applying them effectively, you can build efficient, maintainable, and scalable Python applications for modern development.

CHAPTER 16

WORKING WITH CONTAINERS AND VIRTUAL ENVIRONMENTS

Containers and virtual environments are crucial tools for modern Python development, enabling you to package and isolate applications, manage dependencies, and deploy apps in different environments with consistency. This chapter will explore how to use **Docker** and **Kubernetes** to deploy Python applications, manage dependencies with **virtualenv** and **pipenv**, and provide real-world examples of containerizing Python applications for production.

Using Docker and Kubernetes to Deploy Python Applications

1. **Docker**:

    o **Docker** is a tool designed to make it easier to create, deploy, and run applications by using containers. Containers allow you to package an application with all the dependencies it needs and run it consistently across various environments.

    o **Docker Containers** provide a lightweight alternative to traditional virtual machines and are often used for microservices architectures,

175

simplifying   deployment,   scaling,   and
management.

Steps for Dockerizing a Python Application:

3.   **Create a `Dockerfile`**: A `Dockerfile` contains
instructions on how to build the Docker image for your Python
application. It defines the base image, dependencies, and
commands to run the app.

Example `Dockerfile` for a Flask App:

```
Dockerfile

# Use the official Python image from Docker
Hub
FROM python:3.9-slim

# Set the working directory in the
container
WORKDIR /app

# the requirements.txt file into the
container
 requirements.txt .

# Install the Python dependencies
RUN pip install --no-cache-dir -r
requirements.txt
```

```
#  the rest of the application code
  .  .


# Expose the port that the app will run on
EXPOSE 5000


# Define the command to run the app
CMD ["python", "app.py"]
```

o **Build the Docker Image**:

o In the terminal, run the following command to build the Docker image from your `Dockerfile`:

```bash
docker build -t my-python-app .
```

3. **Run the Docker Container**:

o After building the image, you can run the container with the following command:

```bash
docker run -p 5000:5000 my-python-app
```

This command will start the container and map port 5000 from the container to port 5000 on your machine, allowing you to access your Python app via `http://localhost:5000`.

2. **Kubernetes**:

   ○ **Kubernetes** is an open-source container orchestration platform that automates the deployment, scaling, and management of containerized applications. It is particularly useful when dealing with multiple containers in large, distributed systems.

   ○ Kubernetes manages containers through a cluster of nodes and ensures that containers are running as expected, auto-scaling when necessary.

Steps for Deploying a Python Application to Kubernetes:

0. **Create a Docker Image for Your Python App** (as shown above).

1. **Push the Docker Image to a Container Registry** (e.g., Docker Hub, AWS ECR, or Google Container Registry).

2. **Create a Kubernetes Deployment**: A deployment in Kubernetes defines the desired state of your application (e.g., how many replicas of your app should be running).

Example Kubernetes Deployment Configuration (deployment.yaml):

yaml

```yaml
apiVersion: apps/v1
kind: Deployment
metadata:
  name: my-python-app
spec:
  replicas: 3  # Number of instances of
your app
  selector:
    matchLabels:
      app: my-python-app
  template:
    metadata:
      labels:
        app: my-python-app
    spec:
      containers:
      - name: my-python-app
        image:     mydockerhubusername/my-
python-app:latest
        ports:
        - containerPort: 5000
```

4. **Create a Service to Expose the App**: A **Kubernetes Service** exposes your app to the

outside world. This is often used with a LoadBalancer or Ingress to route external traffic.

Example Kubernetes Service Configuration (service.yaml):

```yaml
apiVersion: v1
kind: Service
metadata:
  name: my-python-app
spec:
  selector:
    app: my-python-app
  ports:
    - protocol: TCP
      port: 80
      targetPort: 5000
  type: LoadBalancer
```

5. **Deploy the Application to Kubernetes**: To deploy the application, use the following commands:

```bash
kubectl apply -f deployment.yaml
kubectl apply -f service.yaml
```

Kubernetes will automatically manage the deployment, scale your application, and expose it through the specified service.

Managing Dependencies and Environments with Virtualenv and Pipenv

1. **Virtualenv**:
   o **virtualenv** is a tool for creating isolated Python environments. It allows you to create environments with specific versions of Python and libraries, ensuring that your project dependencies do not conflict with those of other projects.

   Steps for using `virtualenv`:

2. Install virtualenv:

   bash

   ```
   pip install virtualenv
   ```

3. Create a new virtual environment:

   bash

   ```
   virtualenv myenv
   ```

181

4. Activate the virtual environment:

- On macOS/Linux:

```bash

source myenv/bin/activate
```

- On Windows:

```bash

myenv\Scripts\activate
```

5. Install dependencies within the virtual environment:

```bash

pip install flask    # Or any other
dependency
```

6. Deactivate the virtual environment when done:

```bash

deactivate
```

2. **Pipenv**:

   o **Pipenv** is a higher-level tool that manages both virtual environments and dependencies. It automatically creates and manages a `Pipfile` for managing project dependencies, and a `Pipfile.lock` for ensuring that the correct versions of dependencies are installed.

Steps for using `pipenv`:

1. Install pipenv:

    ```bash
    pip install pipenv
    ```

2. Install dependencies and create a virtual environment:

    ```bash
    pipenv install flask
    ```

3. Activate the environment:

    ```bash
    pipenv shell
    ```

4. To install additional dependencies:

    ```bash
    ```

```
pipenv install requests
```

5. To exit the environment:

```
bash
```

```
exit
```

Pipenv ensures that your dependencies are managed in an organized way, and the `Pipfile.lock` guarantees consistency across different environments.

Real-World Examples of Containerizing Python Applications for Production

1. **Real-Time Chat Application with Flask and Docker**:
    o A real-time chat application built using **Flask** and **Flask-SocketIO** can be containerized using Docker for easy deployment. Using Docker, you can package the entire Flask app, including the **Socket.IO** server, dependencies, and configurations, into a single container that can be deployed anywhere.

Steps:

184

2.   Build the Flask app with Flask-SocketIO.

3.   Create a `Dockerfile` to containerize the app.

4.   Build and run the Docker container.

2. **Data Processing Pipeline with Python and Kubernetes**:

   o   A data processing pipeline built using **Python** (e.g., for ETL processing) can be containerized and deployed using **Kubernetes**. By deploying the pipeline as multiple microservices, Kubernetes can manage scaling, fault tolerance, and resource allocation automatically.

   o   **Example**: A web scraping microservice that collects data, stores it in a database, and then another service processes the data for analytics, all running in isolated containers.

3. **Machine Learning Model Deployment with Docker and Kubernetes**:

   o   Deploying a machine learning model as a microservice using **Flask** or **FastAPI** and Docker allows you to easily containerize the model, serve predictions, and scale the service as needed. With **Kubernetes**, you can orchestrate multiple instances of the model server to handle increased traffic.

   Steps:

185

1. Train the machine learning model.
2. Create a REST API using **Flask** or **FastAPI** to serve the model.
3. Dockerize the application and deploy it to Kubernetes.

Conclusion

Containers and virtual environments are key to managing, deploying, and scaling Python applications. **Docker** enables you to package your application and its dependencies into a portable container, while **Kubernetes** helps manage containers at scale. Using tools like **virtualenv** and **pipenv** to manage dependencies ensures that your applications are isolated and have consistent environments across different machines. Whether you're deploying small apps or large-scale microservices, containerization and proper dependency management are crucial for modern Python development.

CHAPTER 17

BEST PRACTICES FOR WRITING MAINTAINABLE PYTHON CODE

Writing maintainable code is essential to ensure that software remains scalable, understandable, and easy to modify as requirements evolve. In this chapter, we'll explore best practices for code organization, documentation, naming conventions, refactoring, and how to maintain code quality over time. We'll also review real-world examples of refactoring legacy Python code to improve its maintainability.

Code Organization, Documentation, and Naming Conventions

1. **Code Organization**:
   - o **Modularization**: Break your code into small, reusable modules that have well-defined responsibilities. Each module should focus on a single aspect of the application.
     - Use Python's **packages** (directories with an `__init__.py` file) and **modules** (Python files) to structure your project logically.

187

o **Separation of Concerns**: Keep business logic, data access, and presentation (e.g., Flask views, HTML) separate. This will make your code easier to modify and test.

o **Directory Structure**: Adopt a clear and scalable directory structure for your project. Here's an example:

markdown

```
my_project/
├── app/
│    ├── __init__.py
│    ├── models.py
│    ├── views.py
│    └── controllers.py
├── tests/
│    ├── test_models.py
│    └── test_views.py
├── requirements.txt
├── Dockerfile
└── README.md
```

2. **Documentation**:

o **Docstrings**: Use Python's **docstrings** to document functions, classes, and modules. Good docstrings explain the purpose of the code and provide information on parameters, return values, and exceptions.

Example:

```python
def add(a, b):
    """
    Add two numbers and return the result.

    Parameters:
    a (int or float): The first number.
    b (int or float): The second number.

    Returns:
    int or float: The sum of a and b.
    """
    return a + b
```

- o **README Files**: Always provide a **README.md** file that describes the project, its setup, and how to use it. This helps new developers understand the context of the codebase quickly.

- o **In-line Comments**: Use in-line comments sparingly to explain complex code. However,

189

don't overuse comments—write clear, self-explanatory code.

3. **Naming Conventions**:
   - ○ **Follow PEP 8**: Python's official style guide, **PEP 8**, outlines naming conventions and other coding standards. It includes recommendations such as:
     - **Variables**: `snake_case`
     - **Functions and Methods**: `snake_case`
     - **Classes**: `CamelCase`
     - **Constants**: `UPPERCASE_SNAKE_CASE`
   - ○ **Descriptive Names**: Use descriptive, meaningful names for functions, variables, and classes. Avoid single-letter names (except for loop counters or indices).

Example:

```python

def     calculate_total_price(item_price,
tax_rate):
    total = item_price + (item_price *
tax_rate)
    return total
```

Refactoring and Code Reviews: How to Maintain Code Quality Over Time

1. **Refactoring**:

- o **What is Refactoring?**: Refactoring is the process of restructuring existing code to improve its design, readability, and performance without changing its external behavior.

- o **When to Refactor?**: Refactor code when:
  - Code is difficult to understand or maintain.
  - You notice duplicated code.
  - You need to optimize performance or structure.

- o **Principles of Refactoring**:
  - **Small, incremental changes**: Make small, testable changes one at a time to avoid introducing bugs.
  - **Avoiding big-bang refactoring**: Refactor gradually, ensuring the system works after each change.
  - **Automated tests**: Always run tests to ensure that your refactoring doesn't break functionality.

Example: Refactoring a Complex Function:

Before refactoring:

python

```python
def process_data(data):
    processed_data = []
    for item in data:
        if item['type'] == 'type1':
            item['value'] = item['value']
* 2
        elif item['type'] == 'type2':
            item['value'] = item['value']
* 3
        else:
            item['value'] = item['value']
* 4
        processed_data.append(item)
    return processed_data
```

After refactoring:

python

```python
def process_type1(item):
    item['value'] *= 2
    return item

def process_type2(item):
    item['value'] *= 3
    return item

def process_type3(item):
```

192

```
        item['value'] *= 4
        return item

def process_data(data):
    processed_data = []
    for item in data:
        if item['type'] == 'type1':

processed_data.append(process_type1(item)
)
        elif item['type'] == 'type2':

processed_data.append(process_type2(item)
)
        else:

processed_data.append(process_type3(item)
)
    return processed_data
```

The refactored code is now cleaner and follows the **Single Responsibility Principle (SRP),** where each function handles one specific task.

2. **Code Reviews**:

   o **Importance of Code Reviews**: Code reviews are crucial to maintaining high code quality. They help catch potential bugs, improve code quality, and allow for shared knowledge across the team.

- o **Best Practices for Code Reviews**:
  - **Focus on the code, not the person**: Provide constructive feedback that aims to improve the code, not criticize the developer.
  - **Keep reviews small**: Review small chunks of code at a time to ensure focus and efficiency.
  - **Consistency**: Ensure the code follows the project's style guidelines and conventions.
  - **Test-driven development (TDD)**: Ensure that the code has adequate test coverage and passes all tests before merging.

Example of Code Review Comments:

python

```
# Suggestion: Consider extracting the
repeated code into a separate function for
readability.
# It's also a good idea to handle the case
when 'item' doesn't contain the expected
keys.
```

Example of a code review workflow:

3. Submit a pull request with the proposed changes.

    4. Reviewers leave comments and suggestions.

    5. Developer makes adjustments and addresses feedback.

    6. Run automated tests to ensure no functionality was broken.

    7. Merge the changes once they meet the quality standards.

Real-World Examples of Refactoring Legacy Python Code for Maintainability

1. **Refactoring Legacy Monolithic Code**:

    o   **Scenario**: A Python application has grown too large, and different components (e.g., database handling, business logic, and presentation) are tightly coupled, making it difficult to manage and scale.

    o   **Solution**: Refactor the monolithic code into smaller modules or classes, focusing on **separation of concerns**.

    Before Refactoring:

```python
def process_request(request):
    if request['type'] == 'GET':
```

195

```python
        # Retrieve data from the database
        db_data                        =
database.get(request['id'])
        # Prepare the data
        processed_data                 =
process_data(db_data)
        # Format the response
        return
format_response(processed_data)
    elif request['type'] == 'POST':
        # Save data to the database
        result                         =
database.save(request['data'])
        return format_response(result)
    else:
        return        format_error('Invalid
request type')
```

After Refactoring:

```python
python

class Database:
    def get_data(self, id):
        # Retrieve data from the database
        return get_data_from_db(id)

    def save_data(self, data):
        # Save data to the database
        return save_data_to_db(data)
```

```python
class DataProcessor:
    @staticmethod
    def process_data(data):
        return process_data_logic(data)


class ResponseFormatter:
    @staticmethod
    def format_response(data):
        return
format_data_as_response(data)


def    process_get_request(request,    db,
processor, formatter):
    db_data = db.get_data(request['id'])
    processed_data                          =
processor.process_data(db_data)
    return
formatter.format_response(processed_data)


def    process_post_request(request,    db,
formatter):
    result = db.save_data(request['data'])
    return
formatter.format_response(result)


def process_request(request):
    db = Database()
    processor = DataProcessor()
```

```python
    formatter = ResponseFormatter()
    if request['type'] == 'GET':
        return
process_get_request(request,          db,
processor, formatter)
    elif request['type'] == 'POST':
        return
process_post_request(request,          db,
formatter)
    else:
        return          format_error('Invalid
request type')
```

After refactoring, the code is now more modular, easier to test, and more maintainable.

2. **Refactoring Large Functions**:
   - **Scenario**: A function has grown too large, making it difficult to read and maintain. It has multiple responsibilities and includes nested loops and conditionals.
   - **Solution**: Break the function into smaller, purpose-specific functions.

Before Refactoring:

```python
python

def process_data(data):
```

```
for item in data:
    if item['type'] == 'type1':
        item['value'] = item['value']
* 2
    elif item['type'] == 'type2':
        item['value'] = item['value']
* 3
    else:
        item['value'] = item['value']
* 4
return data
```

After Refactoring:

```
python

def process_type1(item):
    item['value'] *= 2
    return item

def process_type2(item):
    item['value'] *= 3
    return item

def process_type3(item):
    item['value'] *= 4
    return item

def process_data(data):
    processed_data = []
```

199

```python
for item in data:
    if item['type'] == 'type1':

processed_data.append(process_type1(item)
)
        elif item['type'] == 'type2':

processed_data.append(process_type2(item)
)
        else:

processed_data.append(process_type3(item)
)
    return processed_data
```

This refactoring improves readability and maintainability by following the **Single Responsibility Principle**.

Conclusion

Writing maintainable Python code is essential for long-term project success. By following best practices for **code organization**, **documentation**, **naming conventions**, and **refactoring**, you can ensure that your codebase remains clean, modular, and easy to maintain. Regular **code reviews** and **automated testing** help maintain code quality over time. Refactoring legacy Python code and improving its maintainability is crucial for adapting to changing requirements and ensuring that the code remains scalable and robust.

CHAPTER 18

THE FUTURE OF PYTHON AND ADVANCED TECHNIQUES

Python has seen explosive growth over the past decade, evolving from a language favored by hobbyists and educators to one of the most widely used programming languages in the world. In this chapter, we'll explore emerging trends in Python development, the future of the language, and key areas where Python is poised for growth, such as **Artificial Intelligence (AI)**, **Internet of Things (IoT)**, and **Quantum Computing**. We will also discuss real-world applications of Python in cutting-edge technologies.

Emerging Trends in Python Development and the Future of the Language

1. **Growing Popularity of Python**:
    - Python continues to top developer surveys and programming language rankings due to its ease of use, extensive library ecosystem, and versatility. Python is being adopted across a wide range of industries—from startups to large enterprises—due to its efficiency and power.

202

o As Python becomes the de facto language for **data science, web development, automation,** and **scripting,** we can expect continued widespread adoption and contributions from the global developer community.

2. **Python in Data Science and Artificial Intelligence**:

   o **AI and Machine Learning (ML)** have become major fields of interest, and Python plays a central role in both. With libraries like **TensorFlow, PyTorch, scikit-learn,** and **Keras,** Python has established itself as the go-to language for AI and ML.

   o In the coming years, Python will continue to evolve to meet the demands of these fields, especially with **deep learning, natural language processing (NLP),** and **AI-driven automation** on the rise.

3. **Python's Role in Cloud Computing**:

   o Python's integration with cloud platforms like **AWS, Google Cloud,** and **Microsoft Azure** is expanding. As more companies move to the cloud, Python's role in **serverless architectures, microservices,** and **cloud-based machine learning solutions** will only grow.

   o Python frameworks like **FastAPI** are becoming increasingly popular for developing high-performance APIs and services that run in cloud environments.

4. **Python for Automation and DevOps**:

   o As DevOps continues to gain momentum, Python's popularity in **automation** is increasing. Developers are using Python to automate repetitive tasks, configure cloud infrastructure, and manage deployments.

   o With tools like **Ansible**, **Fabric**, and **SaltStack**, Python has become a key player in the DevOps automation ecosystem.

5. **Python 3.x and Its Continuous Improvement**:

   o The shift from **Python 2.x** to **Python 3.x** is nearly complete, and Python 3 continues to improve with each release. Upcoming features like **pattern matching** (introduced in Python 3.10) will further enhance Python's functionality and usability.

   o The Python Software Foundation (PSF) is actively working on optimizing performance, introducing async features, and making Python more efficient for modern workloads.

Key Areas of Growth: Artificial Intelligence, Internet of Things (IoT), and Quantum Computing

1. **Artificial Intelligence (AI)**:

- o Python is already the most widely used language for AI, machine learning, and data analysis, thanks to its simplicity and rich ecosystem of libraries.
- o **AI and ML Frameworks**: Python frameworks like **TensorFlow**, **PyTorch**, and **scikit-learn** are integral to building sophisticated AI models for tasks such as image recognition, natural language processing, and autonomous systems.
- o **Deep Learning and Neural Networks**: With Python's advanced capabilities, the development of deep learning models, including **CNNs** (Convolutional Neural Networks) for image processing and **RNNs** (Recurrent Neural Networks) for sequential data, is becoming more efficient and accessible.

Example in AI:

```python
import tensorflow as tf
from tensorflow import keras

# Load the MNIST dataset
(train_images,            train_labels),
(test_images,       test_labels)       =
keras.datasets.mnist.load_data()
```

205

```python
# Build a simple neural network
model = keras.Sequential([
    keras.layers.Flatten(input_shape=(28,
28)),
    keras.layers.Dense(128,
activation='relu'),
    keras.layers.Dense(10,
activation='softmax')
])

model.compile(optimizer='adam',
loss='sparse_categorical_crossentropy',
metrics=['accuracy'])

# Train the model
model.fit(train_images,      train_labels,
epochs=5)

# Evaluate the model
test_loss,           test_acc           =
model.evaluate(test_images, test_labels)
print(f"Test accuracy: {test_acc}")
```

This example showcases Python's central role in AI
by building and training a simple machine learning
model using **TensorFlow** to recognize handwritten
digits (MNIST dataset).

2. Internet of Things (IoT):

- o Python is a popular choice for IoT development due to its simplicity, extensive libraries, and support for low-power devices like **Raspberry Pi** and **MicroPython**.

- o With IoT, Python enables developers to create solutions for smart homes, industrial automation, and connected devices. Libraries like **MQTT** (for messaging), **RPi.GPIO** (for Raspberry Pi hardware control), and **Adafruit CircuitPython** make Python ideal for IoT projects.

Example of IoT with Raspberry Pi:

```python
import RPi.GPIO as GPIO
import time

GPIO.setmode(GPIO.BCM)
GPIO.setup(18, GPIO.OUT)

try:
    while True:
        GPIO.output(18, GPIO.HIGH)  # Turn
on the LED
        time.sleep(1)
```

207

```
        GPIO.output(18, GPIO.LOW)   # Turn
off the LED
        time.sleep(1)
except KeyboardInterrupt:
    GPIO.cleanup()
```

This simple code controls an LED connected to a **Raspberry Pi** using **Python**, showcasing Python's use in physical computing for IoT applications.

3. **Quantum Computing**:
   - Although still in the early stages of development, **quantum computing** is expected to revolutionize industries by solving problems that are currently intractable for classical computers.
   - Python plays a key role in quantum computing, with libraries such as **Qiskit** (developed by IBM) and **Cirq** (developed by Google) making it possible to write quantum algorithms in Python.

Example with Qiskit:

```python
from qiskit import QuantumCircuit, Aer, execute

# Create a quantum circuit with 1 qubit
```

```
qc = QuantumCircuit(1, 1)

# Apply a Hadamard gate to the qubit
qc.h(0)

# Measure the qubit
qc.measure(0, 0)

# Simulate the circuit
simulator                              =
Aer.get_backend('qasm_simulator')
result = execute(qc, simulator).result()

# Print the result of the measurement
print(result.get_counts())
```

This example demonstrates Python's role in quantum computing by using **Qiskit** to simulate a simple quantum circuit and measure its output.

Real-World Applications of Python in Cutting-Edge Technologies

1. **Self-Driving Cars (Autonomous Vehicles)**:
   o **Python** is a core language in the development of self-driving car technologies. Libraries like **TensorFlow** and **OpenCV** are used to process images from cameras and sensors to help cars "see" their environment and make decisions.

209

- o **Waymo, Tesla**, and other autonomous driving companies use Python to build the software stack that powers self-driving cars.

2. **Robotics and AI-powered Robots**:
   - o Python plays an essential role in **robotics**, particularly in building AI-powered robots that can navigate their environment, recognize objects, and perform tasks.
   - o Libraries like **PyRobot** and **ROS (Robot Operating System)**, which uses Python for scripting and automation, make it easier to develop robots with advanced capabilities.

3. **Blockchain and Cryptocurrency**:
   - o Python is frequently used to build blockchain applications and cryptocurrency platforms due to its simplicity and ease of integration with blockchain frameworks like **Ethereum** and **Hyperledger**.
   - o Python libraries like **web3.py** are used to interact with blockchain networks, create smart contracts, and facilitate cryptocurrency transactions.

4. **Natural Language Processing (NLP)**:
   - o Python is the dominant language for **Natural Language Processing**, used in everything from chatbots to search engines. Libraries like **spaCy**, **NLTK**, and **transformers** (for models like GPT

and BERT) allow Python developers to process and understand human language.

- o **Sentiment analysis, chatbots,** and **text summarization** are real-world applications of Python in NLP.

5. **Financial Technology (FinTech):**
   - o Python is heavily used in **FinTech** applications such as fraud detection, algorithmic trading, and financial modeling. Libraries like **pandas, NumPy,** and **QuantLib** are commonly used to analyze and visualize financial data.
   - o **Alpaca,** a commission-free trading platform, and other algorithmic trading platforms provide APIs and Python support to build trading strategies and applications.

Conclusion

Python's future is incredibly bright, with emerging trends in **AI, IoT,** and **Quantum Computing** pushing the boundaries of what is possible with the language. Python continues to evolve to meet the needs of modern developers, offering the tools and frameworks necessary to tackle complex challenges in these cutting-edge fields. As Python continues to grow, its role in **AI development, cloud computing,** and **hardware-based projects** will only increase, solidifying its place as one of the most versatile and valuable languages in the tech ecosystem.

www.ingramcontent.com/pod-product-compliance
Lightning Source LLC
LaVergne TN
LVHW051327050326
832903LV00031B/3406

* 9 7 9 8 3 1 3 6 8 7 1 7 9 *